TEEN ANGST?
NAAAH . . .

ALSO BY NED VIZZINI

Be More Chill

It's Kind of a Funny Story

TEEN ANGST?
NAAAH . . .

A Quasi-Autobiography by
Ned Vizzini

DELACORTE PRESS

All rights reserved. Published in the United States by
Delacorte Press, an imprint of Random House Children's
Books, a division of Random House, Inc., New York. Originally
published in hardcover in the United States by Free Spirit
Publishing, Inc., Minneapolis, Minnesota, in 2000.
Subsequently published in paperback in the United States by
Laurel-Leaf, an imprint of Random House Children's Books,
a division of Random House, Inc., New York, in 2002.

Delacorte Press is a registered trademark and
the colophon is a trademark of Random House, Inc.

Visit us on the Web! www.randomhouse.com/teens
Educators and librarians, for a variety of teaching tools,
visit us at www.randomhouse.com/teachers

Library of Congress Cataloging-in-Publication Data
is available upon request.

ISBN: 978-0-385-73945-0 (tr. pbk.)

Printed in the United States of America

10 9 8 7 6 5 4 3 2 1

First Trade Paperback Edition

To Margaret, for helping raise me.

Thanks to my editors, in reverse chronological order: Elizabeth Verdick, Wendy Lestina, Adam Moss, Andrey Slivka, John Strausbaugh, Sam Sifton, and Mom.

Thanks to Judy Galbraith for telling me to do this book, and then dealing with me as I did it.

Thanks to everybody who shows up in the essays, even if we've since drifted or we no longer speak.

CONTENTS

INTRODUCTION

I started writing this book because of my backpack. I took a bright teal, super-dorky backpack to high school, a backpack my mother had ordered years earlier from L.L. Bean. It worked so great throughout junior high that I figured it had a year or two left in it.

My backpack got some looks. People would stare at it, wondering, "What kind of idiot wears an accessory like that?" Then they would see me. "Oh."

One day, I was going down one of my high school's escalators.* I was tired. I took off my backpack and put it next to me on an escalator step. For whatever reason, the backpack flipped over and started rolling down the escalator like a Slinky.

Many steps below stood a girl. She had one hand to her face, as if she were on a cell phone, but she had no actual cell phone. We were the only people on the escalator. The backpack kept tumbling (I watched it sort of helplessly) and whapped her in the back of the calves.

The girl stopped talking on her fake cell phone

---

*My school had seven sets of escalators. It was a high school specializing in math and science, so I guess they figured we deserved escalators.

and turned to look at me. She had to take that look: I could've been a cute guy who'd flung my backpack at her to break the ice. She sized me up, cocked her head, and kicked my backpack as hard as she could the rest of the way down the escalator.

When I reached the bottom, I picked up my backpack and thought about the incident for the rest of the day. On the subway ride home, I pulled out a wrinkled piece of paper and wrote about the cellphone girl and my stupid bag. I wrote angrily; I used a lot of curses. Afterward, I felt a lot better, and when I read my words the next day, I thought they were pretty good.

So I went from writing profanity-ridden rants to slightly less profanity-ridden essays. I was able to get some of them published in a local newspaper, *New York Press*. Soon I was writing on a regular basis, taking my boring, scary, embarrassing high school moments and turning them into something people could read about. It was a real comfort—if something weird or horrible happened to me, I'd write about it, and then somehow I'd be in control. A little.

A few years later, I got a piece published in *The New York Times Magazine*. That got me in touch with Free Spirit Publishing, who gave me this book contract, which I signed, and now somehow I'm here, writing this introduction after polishing most of what

I wrote in high school and organizing it chrono-logically.

I threw out that backpack when I was a junior and replaced it with a bag from the army surplus store.

I never did learn the name of the girl.

Ned Vizzini
Brooklyn, New York*

* If you want to write to me about my book, you can reach me at www.nedvizzini.com.

JUNIOR HIGH

NINTENDO SAVED ME

Yesterday, on a strange, sudden urge, I hooked up my old Nintendo.* Not the Super NES. The original, spawn-of-the-eighties, from-Japan-with-love, eight-bit Nintendo Entertainment System. It had been lying in a closet for years and was dusty and tough to get working. But when I plugged it in and hit that power button, I was back to being nine years old on the day we bought it.

We went on a Saturday morning after Christmas—my parents always waited for the January sales. Around 8:00 A.M., Dad loaded my six-year-old brother Daniel and me into our van. Our family never had a car, always a van, with two backseats so Daniel and I could space out and not kill each other.

Dad was convinced that Nintendos would be cheaper in New Jersey. He thought everything was cheaper and better in New Jersey, probably because he was born there, in Trenton, which he called "God's Country." We drove to Child World, one of those industrial-sized Toys 'R' Us look-alikes—silent

---

*I had to do that whole Nintendo player's ritual: I blew in the machine until I hyperventilated. I snapped in the game cartridges. I even cleaned the games with Q-tips and alcohol. It took an hour to finish the job.

6

and frigid as a hospital. We headed to the electronics aisle, pulled a Nintendo off the shelf, paid the pimply cashier one hundred dollars (exactly what we would have paid in Manhattan), and drove back to Brooklyn.*

We triumphantly stomped through the front door, shaking snow off our boots. Mom was in the kitchen having breakfast with my sister, Nora. Nora was almost three. She sat on Mom's lap, drank juice from a cup, and scribbled all over *The New York Times* while Mom did the crossword puzzle. Mom loves the *Times* crossword puzzles, especially the ones on Saturday, which are always hardest.** Whenever she finishes one, she writes, "100% Yea Mom" in the margins. It's her thing.

"Daddy's home!" Nora said, jumping out of Mom's lap and hugging Dad's legs. "What is it?" she asked, eagerly looking at the Nintendo box. I held it over my head so she couldn't touch it.

"Jim?" Mom asked from the kitchen, not looking up from her crossword. "You might know this. Ah, Russian river . . ."

"Ob? Volga?"

---

*I lived in an apartment building in Brooklyn from ages seven to eighteen. It was a nice place, but in those eleven years, our family demolished everything: the walls had holes, the beds fell apart, and an electric pencil sharpener in the kitchen somehow became controlled by a dimmer switch in the hall.

**Early in the week, the *Times* crossword puzzles are easy, probably because the editors figure that no one wants to strain themselves on a Monday morning. By Saturday, however, those things are brutal. I can't do one-twentieth of one.

"Volga looks good." Mom penciled in the word. (Later on, when she got even better at cross-words, she'd do them in pen.) "It might not be right, though . . . we'll see. Nora, come back here and finish your juice!"

But now Nora was intrigued. She wanted to know what was in that shiny box. I carried the Nintendo to the living room, sat on the floor, and ravenously tore off all the packaging. Daniel helped. Nora tried to help, but we pushed her away, so she sat on the couch with her stuffed animals.*

Even before she was two, my sister had invented an entire universe of stuffed animals. There were dozens—penguins, dolphins, rabbits—and they all had names that ended in *ee:* Pinky, Yellowy, Mazie, Popsy. They sat on the couch in silent witness as Dad came in, took off his shoes, and announced that he would now assemble the Nintendo.

This required his full concentration, so he told Daniel and me to go play. Hopeful and extremely obedient, for once, we sat on the couch with Nora as Dad connected wires. Within ten minutes, he had the thing working. Dad was a wizard back then.

"I got first game!" Daniel and I yelled simultane-

*As she got older, Nora became extremely protective of her stuffed animals. If you sat on one, she'd make you go to "jail," which meant you had to stand in a corner while she counted to thirty.

ously. I got it, of course. I was the oldest, and the oldest brothers get everything—that's why we're racked with guilt. For half an hour, Daniel watched, and then he started crying, which prompted a visit from Mom.

"What's this machine for? To make you cry?!"

"No, Mom," I moaned.

Daniel shrieked, "Mom, Ned won't let me play! He won't even let me have *one game!*"

"My goodness, Jim, *how* could you buy this? It's like having another TV!" Mom threw up her hands.

"Well, Emma," Dad said from his chair, "it keeps them quiet. They'll sit and gape at it all day."

Now Daniel was playing. That made me mad. I grabbed the controller; he grabbed it back. I hit him and accidentally toppled the Nintendo. It slid behind the TV.

"*Aaa!* Dad! Get it out! *Get it out!*" I screamed. "What if it's broken?" I sobbed.

Dad pulled out the Nintendo and hit the switch. It worked.

"Don't ever do that again," I told Daniel.

"Don't you *ever* tell your brother what to do!" Mom roared from the kitchen.

Nora scampered off the couch. "My stuffed animals don't like fighting, and they're having a *tea party!*" She picked up Pinky, Whitey, Posey, and whoever and ran to her room.

"Okay, *shhh*," Dad said to me, putting his hand on my shoulder. "Let's not fight over the Nintendo. We don't need to make Mom mad, and we don't need to scare Nora, do we? Go on, just gape at that screen and be happy."

So I did. For the next five years.

• • •

I first witnessed a Nintendo upstairs at my neighbor Todd's apartment. Todd, a Cool Kid, was a couple of years older than me. He always got the good toys first. I was instantly awestruck by his Nintendo; like television, it had the power to make you *happy*. Todd could plunk down in front of it anytime, play for a few hours, and be giddy when he stopped. He told me, "Nintendo's even better than TV, 'cause you can win."

Todd was right. Nobody wins at television. If you waste your life watching it, you'll end up on a nursing home couch, glued to a talk show, wondering, "What's it all worth?" But if you waste your life playing video games, you can stand up at the end and yell, "Yes! 500,000 points in Tetris!"* Video games give you purpose.

*Invented by Alexey Pajitnov, Tetris remains the best-loved video game of all time. It's a puzzle game; you arrange falling blocks to score points. Dad loves it as much as Mom loves crosswords. There's actually a whole interesting story behind the game, involving a licensing rip-off and the Soviet government. To learn more, check out: http:atarihq.com/tsr/special/tetrishist.html.

And I was a smart, purposeful kid. When adults asked me what I wanted to be when I grew up, I said, "A cartographer or a civil engineer." Those professions were specific enough to sound smart but vague enough to conceal my real career goal: playing video games.

From ages nine to fourteen, Nintendo was my sole ambition, my prime motivation, and my best friend. I adopted a grueling schedule:

7:30—Wake up and sneak in a game before school.

8:15–3:00—Trudge through school, mumbling, "Boring, boring, boring" while walking the halls.*

3:20—Run home, place my bony butt on the living room floor, and indulge for a few hours.

6:30—Mom gets home. Do my homework, rewarding each finished assignment with a few games.

9:30—Climb into bed and discuss game strategy with Daniel. Fall asleep.

I even dreamed Nintendo. Sometimes I was Mega Man, clad in a blue jumpsuit, with a spherical helmet and a gun for a right arm. Other times, I was in Final Fantasy, the video role-playing game, slaying and getting slain by ogres. I was never Mario: Rebecca, the

---

* I was bored with school from third grade on. What I heard in class was just too far behind what Dad taught me in our one-on-one tutoring sessions. He used to sit me down at the dining room table every evening: "Tonight, son, we're going to learn about atoms. . . ."

prettiest girl in my class, had told me that Mario was "stubby," and I learned early on that this was a bad thing.

Mario, of course, was the short, fat Italian guy who starred in countless Nintendo games. His mission was always to save The Princess, a blond girl with a pink dress and large breasts. She looked kind of like Rebecca. In fourth grade, I picked The Princess as "the girl I would go on a date with if I absolutely had to 'cause everyone else in the world was dead." I spent hundreds of hours saving The Princess. All that time, head aching, palms sweating, butt falling asleep—I'm a little ashamed of it now.

But only a little. You see, childhood sucks. I'm young enough to remember that. Starting in first grade, there's pressure from all sides: to be smart, to make friends, to get teachers to like you. Kids develop different ways of coping with that pressure. Some find solace in books. Some play-act or play large and expensive musical instruments.* Others draw, or sing, or do math. Some watch TV or sit and stare. I coped with childhood by playing Nintendo.

Now, it's been a few years since I've curled up with a jumbo toy catalog and drooled over the video games. When Nintendo 64 (the big next-generation

*I played saxophone for three years, until I left the thing on the subway. I played piano for a year, until I realized I hated it. I've played bass guitar for nine years—and counting—because it looks cool.

system) was released, I didn't even care. Still, I have this future scene all worked out: me, age forty-plus, fat,* and balding, waiting at a bus stop or some other nondescript place. I start daydreaming and humming, and soon I'm whistling the theme to Super Mario Brothers. And the guy next to me, a lanky guy with a beard—he whistles, too.

*I'm skinny now, but over 50 percent of American men end up overweight, so I'll probably be fat later on.

THE TEST

There's a window of time, after you've shed the pathetic dreams of childhood but before the hormones kick in, when you really can do anything. The summer I was thirteen, I wasn't worried about sex or status or pimples. I was worried about the Specialized Science High School Admissions Test.

The test (SSHSAT for short) is a New York City* phenomenon. Here's how it works: the NYC public school system has three "special" high schools for mathematically gifted students—Brooklyn Tech, Bronx Science, and, in Manhattan, Stuyvesant. Parents and students alike covet admission to these schools, because they're free and they don't suck. To separate the gifted kids from the not-so-gifted, the school system issues the SSHSAT, a sort of mini SAT multiple-choice test, scored from 200 to 800. Each school has a different cutoff grade. If you score above the cutoff, you're in. Since Stuyvesant always has the

---

*New York City has five boroughs: Brooklyn, The Bronx, Manhattan, Queens, and Staten Island. Manhattan is the New York of the movies, Queens is where the airports are, Staten Island is at the other end of the ferry, The Bronx has Yankee Stadium, and Brooklyn is where I live. Hope that helps.

highest cutoff, it's the most desirable school. So the thousands of kids who take the SSHSAT each year call it "The Stuy Test."

Anyway, in late May of seventh grade, my class gathered in the math room to hear an announcement from our principal, Mary. (It was a small private school. We called our teachers and administrators by their first names.)

"Now, everybody," Mary addressed us. I was slouched at a table chewing a pencil; I liked the way it tasted. "Your seventh grade is almost over. It's time to start thinking about eighth grade. And when you think about eighth grade, you have to think about high school."

High school. Geez. I chewed vigorously. I never thought I'd get to high school, but now that it was in sight, I started planning. I wanted to conquer high school the way I had conquered elementary school. I wanted to be the smartest student and get the highest grades, because I needed something to feel good about.

Mary continued. "High school is an important step in your life. You'll all be going to different schools, schools that reflect your interests."

I chewed harder, flattening the eraser. Interests, whatever—I wanted to go to the *best* school.

"Getting into these schools is a complicated

process. What you have to do over the summer is think about where you'd like to go, why you'd like to go there, and how you can get yourself admitted. Yes, Josh?"

The questions began. Every kid had some request: where should I go if I like acting? art? movies? law? I had only one question. After class, I caught up with Mary in the hall.

"Mary, do you think I should take the Stuy Test?" I'd taken standardized tests before, and they'd all been easy. I always broke the ninety-eighth percentile; I never had to study. I wanted to know if the Stuy Test would be any different.

"Sure, Ned," she said. "Buy a book on it. Take a look at it over the summer."

I wrote on a piece of loose-leaf, "Buy Stuy book."

"Ned," Mary leaned in close. "You don't need a list, and you don't need to worry. You'll do fine."

Those words weren't a comfort—they were a challenge. I thought I could do fine; Mary thought I could do fine; I'd damn well better do fine.

So began a summer singularly devoted to getting into Stuyvesant. It started with the book. That evening, I trotted into the living room and told my parents I needed it.

"The Stuy Test? Neddy, you'll do just fine. You don't need a book," Mom said.

"He wants a book, I'll get him a book," said Dad.

The following weekend, he took me to a mega-bookstore and we headed for the test-prep section. There it was, sitting low on a rotating display case, light gray with blue letters: *Preparing for the SSHSAT: 8 Practice Exams Included!*

"That the one?" Dad asked.

"Yup." I smiled, stowed the book under my pre-pubescent armpit, and walked to the cashier past some blurry-eyed high school kids scanning SAT books. "That's me in four years," I thought.

I went home and cracked open the book, eager to start on the problems. I read the first one: "A circle with diameter 4 has an area of ? Use $\pi= 3.14$." I reread it. Was this some kind of joke? I hadn't *done* pi before. I ran to show Mom.

"Mom! Mom! How do you do this?"

My ears were hot. My stomach was knotted around my throat.

"Calm down, Ned, calm down."

She sat me down at the dining room table. "Ned, I saw this coming. Ever since you heard about this test, you have been *too worried*. Understand? You are *not allowed* to obsess about this test. Understand?"

"Yeah."

But it was too late. I was already obsessed. The

test had offended me by giving me questions I couldn't answer. I intended to kill it.

"Now, as for this problem, it's just pi. Do you want me to show you how pi works?"

I nodded. She showed. I'm a fast learner.

I got some index cards and wrote on them in clear seventh-grade print: "Area = πr^2" and "Circumference = $2\pi r$." I taped the cards to the wall near my bed. When I fell asleep that night, the cards were the last things I saw.

The second day, I worked on vocabulary. *Abject* and *knoll* were words I didn't know, so I dug up a book called *The Words You Should Know: 1,200 Essential Words Every Educated Person Should Be Able to Use and Define* and I started with *A*. I worked through *abnegate, abrogate, abstruse, amortize*. I put them on cards, too. I closed my bedroom door. Family was now ancillary to the test.

On the third day, I started making tables. Fractions and decimals. I made two little columns. One read from $\frac{1}{2}$ to $\frac{1}{20}$; the other, .5 to .05. For each fraction, including the weird ones like $\frac{1}{17}$, I wrote the appropriate decimal. I hand-calculated everything in the warm air of my room.

It was mind-numbing work, but that was the point. Studying *is* mind-numbing. There's information on paper, and you shove it into your head. It doesn't involve people, or feelings, or getting others to like you. As I continued to prepare for the Stuy Test, afternoon in, afternoon out, I realized that despite the propaganda, I *liked* studying. I didn't care about what TV told me, and I didn't care what my friends thought—studying was *fun.*

When I went to summer camp,* I took the book. I spent four weeks with wanna-be teen rebels. I was a rebel, too, participating in routine camp activities but in the back of my mind thinking, "$1/_{13} = 0.0769$." At night, if I wasn't too tired, I would turn on my flashlight and quietly test myself. Then I'd slip the book under my pillow, so the information would diffuse into my head overnight.

I worked on triangles, memorizing formulas for base and height. I thought, "Parallelogram, trapezoid, rhombus, rectangle." I put myself far above my campmates, deciding smugly that I wasn't "confused" or "different." I didn't listen to loud music or salivate over girls. I had a test to study for. I was focused on a single, attainable goal.

I left camp with some friends and some enemies, and carried the test-prep book home to the city. These were the worst two weeks of the summer, the real hot, soggy ones in late July. By now, I was up to the *Ds* in *The Words You Should Know. Deign, dema-*

---

*This was the same camp that's detailed on pages 71–78.

gogue, dereliction, discomfit. I started writing a little book that I never finished, offering advice for students taking the Stuy Test.* Flash cards littered the house.

And all the time, I was getting smarter. I knew pi; I knew graphs. I knew mean, median, and mode. I knew $1/12 = .0833$. I knew the vocabulary through *E*. There is a movie called *Stand and Deliver* where an overachieving teacher shows underprivileged high school students calculus in six months. Whenever those students had to get some work done, you'd see clips of them improving, as pop music played in the background. My summer was like *Stand and Deliver* without the pop music.

I took the book with me to Lake George, in upstate New York, on our family vacation. A flubbery** old woman was reading on the beach. The presence of me with a test book annoyed her. She glowered and said, "Whaddaya studying for? This is a beach! Enjoy yourself!"

I grinned. The information was flowing from the paper to my head. Life had never seemed so simple or so right.

---

*Also during this time, I wrote a very bad short story about an old man named Arnold Adams, who didn't need women or family or anything, and lives on his porch shooting at passing cars. It's around somewhere.

**Don't tell me you don't know what *flubbery* means. It's that look old people get when their neck hangs down, and their arms hang down, and they appear to be melting in their own skin.

When that test finally rolled around, it wasn't even an issue. I took it and got into Stuy. It was like building a sand castle—the work was the fun part; the end result was sort of a letdown. As a force of habit, I continued reading *The Words You Should Know* in my freshman year, eventually getting to *S*. I studied very hard throughout my four years at Stuy, but I never approached the superhuman weirdness of that summer.

HIGHWAY TO HELL

My family takes cheap vacations. Any trip that involves an airplane, we avoid—too much money. Any trip that involves a resort, we shun—too many people. Disney World, Busch Gardens, camping, Europe? We'd never consider them. What we do for vacations is pile into our van and drive to weird East Coast destinations, like Binghamton, New York, hometown of *The Twilight Zone* creator Rod Serling. (Seriously. I've been in the Rod Serling *museum*.)

On one of these jaunts, we ended up at the Allentown, Pennsylvania, county fair. We had meant to go to the Poconos, but Dad decided at the last minute that we needed some real culture, so we headed for "The Largest County Fair in Eastern P.A."

The place was full of suburban guys my age, traveling in groups, chatting up girls, and smoking cigarettes. I was being led around by Mom and Dad, with Daniel and Nora in tow. I tried walking fifty feet ahead of my family or trailing far behind them, but the suburban kids were onto me no matter what. They gave me dirty looks and snickered as I passed by.

"Hey, Ned?" Dad asked at a particularly low moment. "How would you like to see that?" I looked where he was pointing—a stadium marquee with red letters:

6 P.M. TONITE COME SEE THE WORLD'S LARGEST DEMOLITION DERBY!!! $5

Destruction can really cheer up a thirteen-year-old. I wasn't sure what a demolition derby was, but it sounded violent and it would give me a chance to stop walking around with my parents. I told Dad, "Sure."

Here's how a derby works: some redneck with a car so screwed up that no one will buy it decides to have fun and compete for prize money. He pays about fifty bucks; his vehicle gets a paint job, and its engine is "modified" so it'll run for a few more hours. On derby day, he drives to a stadium where he slams into other cars until he totals them all, or just his own. If his is the last car running, he gets a big check.

We bought our tickets. "It's just like a baseball game," Mom announced, but she would soon learn.

We entered the stadium—a racetrack used for derbies every other week—through a Colosseum-like stone arch. We went to our seats in the very back of the stands, right in front of two young mothers holding toddlers. We were such tourists: Dad kept checking our tickets ("6Y, 6Y, where *is* 6Y?"), and Mom read off events from the county fair calendar ("Look, kids, tomorrow there's a pig judging!") as we sat down. I rolled my eyes.

"Why are you embarrassed?" Dad asked quietly. "Look around—do you really care what these people think of you?"

I did look around. The stadium was filled with burnt-out blondes, dirty drunks, and thirty-year-old guys with their mothers, but somehow, my family stuck out the most.

I tried to concentrate on the track below. In the middle, on a big concrete island, stood a podium and mike. A bald announcer came out and intoned, "Thank you, folks, for coming to our Saturday evening derby."

The crowd booed. The mothers in back of us booed loudest. Disgusting.

"Ah . . . tonight," the announcer continued, "we have something special for you. Our own Miss Kate Daugherty will sing our national anthem." A tiny girl in a flowered dress minced up to the podium, planted her face too close to the mike, and in a cute but some-how terrible way croaked out "The Star-Spangled Banner."

Without hesitation, the crowd hissed and jeered. Some people even threw soda cans and Styrofoam cups at Miss Daugherty. They didn't hit her—they were too far back in the stands for that—but the girl looked ready to flee, and the announcer quickly hustled her offstage after her song. Mom and Nora were shocked. So was I, outwardly, but part of me sort of liked the booing, and when my parents weren't looking, I did a little myself.*

As the announcer droned on about derby "rules," the cars emerged. There were about thirty of them—two-doors, mostly, with a few four-doors and station wagons. Each car was painted with a number and a name like, "#92, The Avenger." Everyone chose a car to root for. I liked an orange station wagon that had gigantic faces of Beavis and Butt-head** on its side.

The cars formed a circle, front ends facing in. The announcer began the countdown: "Five . . . four . . ."

*Miss Daugherty was much younger than me, and she was doing something better than I ever could do it—that's why I booed. Even in junior high I was hypercompetitive, and I loved it when other people failed. Sorry.

**Beavis and Butt-head were the animated stars of the *Beavis and Butt-head* television show, one of humankind's more accomplished satires. They made fun of teenage television-addicted wasteoid culture by analyzing music videos and setting things on fire.

Engines revved, kicking up smoke. "Three . . . two . . ."

Three rows down, a fat guy lifted his chin to the sky and shouted, *"Yeehah!"*

"One . . . Go!" The screeching of cars and fans melded in a roar.

That Beavis and Butt-head station wagon was the first to die. While the other vehicles charged forward, it vroomed *backward,* smashing into the stadium wall. It was quickly sandwiched by a Pontiac. The Beavismobile's driver jumped through his windshield—the glass had been removed "to prevent injury"—and yelled at his car as it burst into flames. The blaze licked the stadium wall, obscuring other cars, spreading a stench of burnt-rubber smoke.

Derby clowns—like rodeo clowns, except with hoses—ran out and extinguished the fire. Everyone cheered. In another corner, two cars were going at it like mechanical elk: backing up, smashing into each other, backing up again. Each confrontation produced a metallic groan and thick black fumes. Six-year-old Nora was going through her environmental phase. She stood on her seat and yelled, "This is pollution!"

The crowd around us told her to sit the hell down. The mothers in back of us shot especially fiery looks.

Mom had had enough. "Jim," she said. "This is not an appropriate place for children." She grabbed Nora's hand and left the stands. Dad said we'd see her when the derby was over.

By now it was clear: the two best cars were "Dickhead" and "Bonehead." Bonehead was a big old black station wagon, covered with decals of skulls and crossbones. He was a brute; he smashed smaller cars easily. Dickhead—that's what it said right on the side in huge brown letters—was a gray two-door with oversized wheels. The driver was wily; he didn't do much smashing, but he avoided hits and outlasted his competitors. Dickhead and Bonehead seemed to have a pact that they wouldn't clash until all the other cars were out.

There was so much to watch. Number Forty-one lost all its tires and was driving on hubs. Number Twenty-two leaked so much oil that it couldn't move—no traction.* Suddenly the announcer called, "Halftime!" The still-mobile cars were driven to a pit-stop area, where the drivers got out and daintily stretched. Nonmoving cars were towed away to become scrap-metal cubes in a Pennsylvania junkyard.

Halftime began. Two derby clowns, dressed as firemen, drove into the stadium in a little red fire

*A car was officially out of the derby if it didn't move for fifteen seconds. When that time had elapsed, the announcer would pipe up from his booth, "Number Sixty-four, turn off your engine. Don't even try to move. It's *aaaall* over."

truck. They circled the racetrack, tooting a shrill horn and drenching each other with a hose. For a really big laugh, they stuck the hose between their legs and pretended to pee on the crowd. The patrons were not amused. They yelled, "What the hell is this? *Sesame Street*?" and threw empty food containers. The clowns flipped them off and continued their act.

As the clowns did their thing, I muttered something to Dad about how AC/DC* would have made a much better halftime act. This attracted the immediate attention of one of the mothers behind us.

"AC/DC! I love them!"

"Yeah?" I said, turning around. "So do I. I have all the CDs with Bon—"

"Highway to hell!" she began singing, rather well actually, bouncing her toddler on her knee.** "Highway to *hell!* I love that song! Highway to hell! That's my favorite!"

"You know what would be really cool?" Daniel chimed in. I smiled. My little brother looked like a smaller version of me, and he tended to come up with warped ideas like me as well. "It would be really cool

---

*An Australian rock band. What I love most about them is that after their first singer, Bon Scott, met his "death by misadventure" (aka alcohol-related stuff—but seriously, that's on his death certificate), they found another singer who sounded *just* like him and went on to play for three decades and counting.

**AC/DC's best song.

if AC/DC was playing on little harnesses, like, flying over the derby as the cars crashed into each other."

"Wow," one of the mothers said. The other one was still bouncing her child and singing. "That is a really, *really* cool idea."

"Not exactly," I said, challenging my brother. "How are you going to suspend the drummer over a demolition derby?"

"They could suspend the drums, too!"

"Or they could use electronic drums." This from my dad.

"It wouldn't be the same," the singing mother said. "Highway to hell! Dun, dun! It would be a lot better than these clowns, y'know?"

The second half of the derby was the same as the first but drunker—more rowdy cheers, more mangled autos. Four cars remained. Number Twenty-three got blind-sided and whipped around, slamming into Number Sixteen. Sixteen revved his engine too fast, and a piece of tire ripped off and flew across the stadium.

Then, finally, Dickhead and Bonehead faced off. I decided to root for Dickhead—the underdog, the sly trickster, constantly running from danger. Except he didn't always run successfully. Bonehead gave him a few good hits, tore off his bumpers, and crumpled up his hood like a mountain range.

Front end skewed, engine dragging, parts trailing, Dickhead gave one last gasp as his engine fell out. By then, it was no longer even a car—just a heap of metal with three wheels. The announcer thundered, "We *haaaave* a champion!"

A dinky recorded version of the national anthem played over the loudspeakers. The clowns rushed out and presented Bonehead's driver with a nine-hundred-dollar check and a medal. He gave the audience a grimy smile.

The two mothers walked with us out of the stadium, back through that stone arch, rehashing the details of our AC/DC Demolition Derby World Tour.

Daniel: "You could have the whole band playing on a see-through net, like, above the derby."

Mother #1: "I don't think you can stand up or play drums on a net."

Me: "Forget about the drums. We already said electronic drums."

Dad: "I hate electronic drums."

Me: "Who cares?"

We found Mom and Nora, and on our way out of the county fair, I bought a T-shirt that read "35th Annual Destructo-rama Derby." The suburban kids eyed it jealously as I walked behind my family.

ARE WE ALTERNATIVE NOW?

When I was thirteen, I went to my friend Ike's house and formed a band called Wormwhole. I provided percussion (I banged some drumsticks together) and Ike, who thought up the name, played acoustic guitar.

A few things about Ike: First, he's a cool guy, one of my best friends, and I'm privileged to know him. Second, he's a big, buff Mayan dude—he was born in Central America, where, I learned, the Mayans were conquered by the Spanish in 1519,* but he *swears* he has full-on Mayan warrior blood in him. That probably accounts for his workout schedule: Ike's room is a mini gym full of punching bags, weights, and rowing machines, and he constantly uses them. His biceps are as thick as my neck.

Ike is also a vampire enthusiast. He owns a huge collection of vampire books; he has dark robes, teeth, and vampire figurines strewn all over his room. He once told me he really *was* a vampire—he claimed

---

*See? I had to do a little research. Don't let anyone tell you it's easy writing a book.

he'd been abducted as a baby and taught "the ways of the night" in Costa Rica.

To complement his vampire fixation, Ike has a large collection of knives, which he buys from catalogs and keeps in his "Weapons Locker." He also collects more exotic weapons: *bolas, sai,* and *nunchucks.** I started hanging out with him because he was just too weird to pass up. But as I came to know him, I discovered a genuinely kind person with a twisted sense of humor. We've had some fun times.

Once, in eighth grade, Ike and I cut school to protest something called Take Our Daughters to Work Day. We were irked—how come the girls got to visit their parents at work while we toiled over algebra? We made our own signs (mine: "Stop Reverse Sexism!" Ike's: "Help! U R Oppressing Me!") and walked down to Seventh Avenue—the main street of our neighborhood, Park Slope.**

We positioned ourselves in front of a coffee shop and paced in circles, yelling, "Equal rights now! Hey, hey, hey!" Not many people were sympathetic to our cause. In fact, almost everyone ignored us, although

---

*A *bola* is a piece of rope with a heavy ball on each end; you throw it, and it wraps around your target's leg or neck. A *sai* is a three-pronged Japanese dagger. A *nunchuck* is two pieces of wood connected by a short chain. (You may know those last two from *Teenage Mutant Ninja Turtles.*)

**I grew up in Park Slope, Brooklyn. When we first moved there, it was a lesbian neighborhood—I saw more lesbian couples than straight ones. But after a couple of years, the lesbians moved out and the yuppies moved in. By the time I was in eighth grade, it was all coffee shops, video stores, and liberal ideals.

some women rolled their eyes, and one said, "Yeah, like you guys know jack about sexism."

One guy was supportive—he drove by in a pickup truck, leaned out his window, yelled, "All right, fellas! Keep on truckin'," pumped his fist, and drove off. Just when I was starting to think the whole Take Our Daughters to Work Day protest was a big success, our school principal, Mary, showed up. She had come down to Seventh Avenue *in her own car*. She personally drove Ike and me back to school, and then gave us detention for the next six weeks, until graduation.

In detention, we had to compile a report on the mental health of adolescent girls. I read *Reviving Ophelia*, and after sifting through accounts of bulimia, anorexia, and sexual abuse, I decided that teenage girls have it plenty rough; if they wanted to spend a day hanging out at their parents' jobs, more power to them.*

But back to Wormwhole. We recorded two songs in Ike's bedroom, "Pants in the Mail" and "Lumber." They were both instrumentals, because there was no way I was banging the drumsticks together and singing at the same time. Ike was a terrific guitarist. For one thing, he actually had a guitar. For another, he had an instructional video, *How to Play Guitar*

---

*Although I shouldn't have been so wimpy. A few years later, Take Our Daughters to Work Day became Take Our Daughters *and Sons* to Work Day! Coincidence? Well. Probably.

with Dean Hamill, which I borrowed and later lost. He could even tune. He couldn't play chords, but who needs them?

As for percussion, I was solid on those drumsticks. Never missed a beat. I could even solo with them. Each of the songs had a good hook, a development, a solo, and a concluding section. I figured we could make a single, send it to radio stations, and be famous in a few weeks.

For some reason, though, nobody liked our music. I played it for my parents, and they hated it. I played it for my music teacher, and she said, "Don't quit your day job." I played it for other kids, and they gave me a look.* Eventually (i.e., after a couple days), we had to face facts: Wormwhole was a failure.

A few weeks later, though, while watching a music video and feeling misunderstood, I realized something: Wormwhole may have been a failure, but it wasn't bad. And it isn't bad, to this day. It's just *alternative*. There's a fine line between the two, and nobody knows where it is. Wormwhole was an alternative to alternative—our music was so alternative it would blow your mind.

First, we had no amps. Only conformists use amps. Second, we had no vocalist. Everyone's got a

---

*I saw this look a lot in junior high, elementary school, and all the way back to kindergarten. It was the "Ugh, Ned's *talking*" look people gave me when they wanted me to shut up.

vocalist; our lyrics were telepathic. Third, we had only two songs. Why write more? Fourth, parents, teachers, and (conformist) youth hated us—so we must have been good. Fifth, look at the name! Who knows what it means?

For all these reasons, and many more that I'll think up later, you need our demo tape, *Crap (and Lots of It)*. It features "Pants in the Mail" and "Lumber," with five extra-special bonus tracks of me playing bass guitar and singing. The first five people who contact me by any means possible will be allowed to buy a copy. Just think: your parents won't understand your music, your friends won't understand your music—you'll be the most alternative person ever.*

---

*As it happens, several people contacted me about this after the book was originally published. I had to tell them that I lost the demo (it was on cassette). But years later, I popped a blank tape into my tape player to see if it had music on it—and heard some medieval-type chanting, followed by the Wormwhole demo! It was put there by God! I transferred it to a computer and now it is available at nedvizzini.com/fun/#music.

FRESHMAN YEAR

STUY HIGH

When I arrived at Stuyvesant High School on September 9, I was already terrified. I was terrified of high school girls; I was terrified of high school cliques; I was terrified because I'd been told that if you stood near Stuyvesant at 8:00 A.M., the wave of teenagers going to class would trample you. You'd be ground into the ground. I'd heard that some people died that way.

Turned out I didn't need to be so terrified. True, I didn't do too well with those high school girls. And the cliques got on my nerves. But the wave of teenagers going to class became my friends, and I became one of them: head lowered, hood raised, sleepwalking into school with my heavy backpack, like everybody else.

Stuyvesant High School has been called "the crown jewel of the New York City public school system" and "the best high school in America." It's a big, beige, brick place: 3,000 kids, ten stories high, with its own *bridge*. New York politicians decided they didn't need students getting run over on their way to the crown jewel, so they built a bridge over a highway to ensure us safe access. And that's just for starters.

Stuy has a marble lobby with chandeliers straight out of the Plaza Hotel and the school's motto carved in stone: *Pro scienta atque sapienta*.* There are three elevators and seven escalators, the computer rooms have new computers, the halls are fresh and clean, and even the bathrooms sparkle. It's like going to school at Club Med. My dad has a theory that the whole place was financed by the Mafia as a scheme to jack up surrounding property values. It cost one hundred twenty million bucks to build.

THE STUDENTS

I came to school that first day with a sci-fi paperback tucked under my arm. I wasn't the only one. Stuy was full of kids with books; every other person seemed to have one, to defend against social interaction. I saw people going to school reading books, and walking through the halls with their faces buried in books. As the year progressed, the paperbacks gave way to fat textbooks, but the result was the same—everybody had a book.

Besides that, the only common thread among Stuy students was that we'd all passed "The Stuy

Pro scienta atque sapienta means "For science and wisdom." There's a reason I took Latin for four years, man, and it wasn't just to keep me from learning a language that might immerse me in the real world!

Test."* Admission to the school was based solely on a special test called the SSHSAT, given in eighth grade. The test was supposed to keep Stuy chock-full of smart, industrious kids, but somehow that didn't work with my class. We were a random collection of nerds, jocks, geniuses, potheads, drunks, tortured poets, young Republicans, shifty-eyed loners, and just plain idiots. That first day, I met a freshman who was taking calculus and a twenty-two-year-old who still hadn't graduated. I saw girls who looked like they spent all their free time on their hair, and guys who looked like they spent all their free time down at the acne farm. I saw young men who'd stop in the middle of the hall to do one-armed push-ups, and young men who'd scrawled "God Is Gay" in Whiteout on their backpacks.

But beneath all that, everyone at Stuy was *nice*. Even if they snarled and huffed, the seniors didn't beat you up. People mumbled "Sorry" if they bumped into you in the halls; they said "Excuse me" before charging past you on the stairs. Nobody went out of their way to bother you because everyone was incredibly self-motivated. The kids at Stuy cared about *their* grades, *their* problems. I fell quickly into that pattern.

Only a week into my freshman year, my train of

* "The Test" is on pages 14–21.

thought was acting hyperactive. I'd be sprinting to class thinking, "Math, math, did you do it? Yeah, okay, what about English? Are you sure? Oh, wait: *lab!* No, lab's tomorrow, it's okay. . . ." I didn't have *time* to bother anyone else.

And no one else had time to bother me. I would've had to run through the halls naked, covered in chocolate sauce, for any seniors to acknowledge my presence. I came to view that as an advantage. I never had to worry about what others thought of me because they didn't think of me at all. They were concentrating on grades.

GRADES

Stuy gave number grades—84, 92, 100—instead of As and Bs. Every year, the administration talked about switching to a "nicer" grading system: letter grades of E, S, N, U (Excellent, Satisfactory, Needs Improvement, Unsatisfactory) or Pass/Fail. That never happened. Number grades made us work harder, and when we worked harder, we went to Good Colleges, and when we went to Good Colleges, the school's record looked great.

Grades were a touchy subject at Stuy. There was an etiquette about them. As they were handed out, you didn't turn to your friend and ask, "What are your grades?" You asked, "What'd you get?"—putting the blame for a potentially bad grade on the teacher. If you asked someone what they "got," you had to be ready to answer the same question yourself. If you saw someone visibly distraught over their grades, you didn't bug them—it was taboo. And you never, never bragged about what you got.

It was like a ballet, the intricate dance of the grades. Kids didn't bellow "Seventy-five! You suck!" or "Yes! I got a ninety-eight!" But we were all *thinking* those things. We hid our celebration, gloating, and anguish, only revealing ourselves with subtle gestures: a slight smile, a clenched fist.

CLIQUES

The constructive part of the Stuy grade obsession was that it distracted us from our social lives. When you're worrying about physics labs and *David Copperfield,** you don't have time to torture your peers. Stuy's student body wasn't vicious; it was simply separated into distinct groups that hoarded goods, traveled as one, and ostracized others.

First, we had the preppies. The preppies were okay; they had nice clothes, and they didn't smell bad. They all seemed to come from the same junior high school, and they recognized each other instantly on the first day. The girls were small and pretty, the

---

*A book by Charles Dickens. Chapter 1 is "I Am Born."

guys well-built with great hair. The preppies always seemed busy, but you never really knew what they were up to. They would go off in little groups—to eat? hang out? do drugs? have orgies? They'd come back from weekends with amazing stories (so-and-so got arrested, so-and-so performed this act upon so-and-so) that you could neither confirm nor deny. Generally, each preppy did one *non*preppy thing to gain credibility, such as playing in a band or being a graffiti artist.

Speaking of artists, there were those, too: red-eyed, purple-haired poets, guys in turtlenecks, girls with hemp bracelets. These people loved seeing their names in obscure school magazines, and I was jealous of them because they were jaded. I wanted so badly to be jaded at Stuy. I wanted to walk around slumped over, mumbling cynically to myself, proving that even at age fourteen, I'd been there, done that.

There were the wanna-be slackers, too. Preppies with stubble, they had as much money as the rich kids but spent it on skateboards, cigarettes, Rollerblades, punk clothes, and hair dye. One of them wore a name tag that read, "Hello, My Name Is . . . Satan." Like the preppies, who congregated around a Snapple machine by the lobby, the wanna-be slackers had their own hangout: a small concrete ledge called "The

Wall." They stayed out on The Wall during school, playing chess and exchanging snotty small talk.

Stuyvesant also had some great sports teams—in particular our swimming squad, the Penguins, won the city championships almost every year—so we had jocks. I didn't have much contact with them; they were quiet when they weren't hooting, and they generally kept to themselves. I had friends who became jocks, though. They would start the transformation over a period of weeks, spending more and more time after school with the team; then all of a sudden they'd be getting girlfriends and snazzy logo sweatshirts and talking to me in only the most cursory way.

Behind the jocks, artists, nerds, preppies, chess nuts, heavy-metal guys, folksy guitar players, scary kids with black trench coats, neo-Nazis, and what's-his/her-names was the general collection of bozos and rejects that I hung out with. Most of them were Magic players—guys who spent their free time at Stuy playing a fantasy card game called Magic: The Gathering.* We took over a corner of the sixth floor, where we sat on the ground with our cards. We came and went in shifts, playing during our lunch periods, running off to class as the bells rang. We couldn't really remember each other's names so we just yelled, "Hey you, you wanna play?" It was a desperate

*Details of my Magic obsession are on pages 126–130.

44

frenzy, kids playing Magic all the time, thinking about the cards so they wouldn't have to think about anything else.

I didn't only play Magic; between games, I befriended some computer people, some druggies, some music nuts, and some loners. The loners were interesting; they just walked around. No one teased them. No one really noticed them. They just . . . walked around.

THE GRIND

After a week at Stuy, I started hearing about how hard it was to get up in the morning and how "the daily grind is getting to me, man." Once-enthusiastic kids were complaining like whiny forty-year-olds in dead-end jobs.

The workload *was* hard. Freshman year, we had up to three hours of homework each night, and that worsened as time went on. A biology teacher once put it to me this way: "Getting through Stuy is easy. You have three options: good grades, social success, and sleep. You can only have two out of three." I chose grades and sleep. The people who chose grades and social success (getting drunk on the weekends when they should've been studying and whatnot) ended up with some problems. They'd come to school bleary-eyed and sleep in the hallways. But missing sleep was cool—it gave them something to brag about. They'd meet each other and say, "Man, I am so tired. I got, like, twenty hours of sleep this whole week, and I partied all weekend." Response: "Yeah . . . I'm not kidding, man, I have three tests today. I was up studying for bio until four." A war of antisleep bragging rights.

Some days, I went to school on no sleep, but adrenaline got me through. When I took tests, I always got a palpable high—my brain buzzed with endorphins as I stared at those questions. Stuyvesant was a big, exciting place, and just being in the building was a rush for me. I'd walk through the door, no longer a powerless little kid. I was a ninja, prowling the halls in search of good grades.

THAT LEARNING STUFF

Stuyvesant had an interesting take on education. The plan, it seemed, was to cram a student's head full of information, test the student repeatedly, and then move on to an unrelated subject with frightening speed. It was a shock, after studying digestion for a month, to hear your biology teacher announce, "Okay, this unit is over. Forget about the human digestive system. On to locomotion in the paramecium."

But I *did* forget about the human digestive system, and quickly, because it was no longer on the test. Everything at Stuy was either meaningless or on the test. "It's not on the test? Dude, are you serious, she's not testing us on this?" *Smack*. That would be the sound of a textbook closing. If something wasn't on the test, you just closed your book and smiled.

Problem was, even things that weren't on the test could show up on the final. Stuy finals tended to be standardized, so every biology class took an exam written collectively by the biology department. That meant every final included at least one question you couldn't possibly answer because your teacher had screwed up and not taught it. The final exams at Stuy were everything: the products of your labor, the causes of your anxiety, the details that kept you up at night, the challenges that, once met, *oh boy.* School's . . . out . . . for . . . summer! All you had now was a vague sense of dread that you'd messed up and wouldn't get into a Good College.

I went into Stuyvesant High School terrified; I came to think of the place not as a terror, but as a manageable form of pain. Not a sharp, wincing pain that went away quickly—a chronic, dull, four-year ache that, if pressed on the right way, felt kind of good.

FIFTEEN MINUTES

I leave the house at 7:23 every morning. Well, not exactly 7:23—I wish I were that anal—more like 7:25 or :26. I take fifteen minutes (even if I run) to reach the subway. I spend two or three more minutes waiting on the platform. When the train comes, I run to the front car and try to beat out an adult for a seat. I usually fail. Then, I'm faced with the day's first problem: what to do on the way to school. I have fifteen minutes to kill.

Let's start with the obvious: I could read. At 7:45 A.M., a New York subway car is a remarkably literate place. The *Daily News,* the Bible, *Waiting to Exhale,** R. L. Stine, a chemistry textbook—half the straphangers are reading. But I can't read on the train. Invariably, I get caught up in a chapter and lose my balance, falling into the businesswoman next to me, who's also reading. She closes her thick, important-looking book and glares at me. I cringe, shuffle away, and look at the floor. Bumping into men isn't so bad;

---

*A book about women waiting to get into a committed relationship so they can exhale. Very similar to my desires at the time.

they just *harrumph* and turn back to the sports section. Still, reading's out.

I could always fantasize, but come on. Cramped by some overweight banker, smelling b.o. that's just starting to stale, wearing a fifteen-pound backpack, and clutching my math notebook in my teeth, I'm going to think about the woman next to me?

I could scan the passengers, like Dad does. He's always analyzing strangers on the train, building stories around their imagined lives. "See those two? He's an architect, and he loves her, but he can't stand her cats." Never a dull moment for Dad. But I'm no good at crafting urban tales.

I could hum, but this causes problems, too. My humming inevitably leads to openmouthed mumbling, which becomes these horrible "Dun, dun, dada, dun, da" noises, which lead to full-blown, off-key singing in my corner of the subway car. Sometimes I belt out the entire "Spider-Man" theme song ("Is he tough? Listen, bud / He's got radioactive blood") before shutting myself up.

I experimented with a Walkman. I'd put on the headphones, hunch over, and wear a jaded, sullen-teen face as I brooded in the back of the car. But I'm not sullen, and I can't fake it; the Walkman was eventually crushed by an unruly businessman.

Often, the idea of talking with my fellow strap-hangers has crossed my mind. There are two I recognize—the annoying woman with the sunglasses who never gets a seat, and the cute green-haired girl who actually seems intimidated by me. Many times, I've been ready to address them, but I always reconsider and pull out my global notes to study.

I could sleep, but how? A typical subway rider sleeps standing up, chin dropped to the chest, or sitting, head tilted back. These positions never work for me. The only way I can rest is by sitting with my backpack on my lap, and my head on my backpack. Bent forward, covered in my coat and sweatshirt, I look like a twisted midget escaped from rehab. My back gets bent up, and then hurts all day. I never actually fall asleep.

Sometimes, though, I fall half asleep. Being half asleep is terrific; my sense of time slows down, and I picture weird things. Sometimes I press my palms against my eyes on the subway to see whirling tunnels or flashing squares. Once, firmly planted in this zone, I saw a gray machine extruding strawberries through a little nozzle.*

But I can't be half asleep all the time, and I'm running out of options. I could stare and think about mysteries of the cosmos. Let's see . . . *Is there a God?*

---

*The strawberry image was crystal clear to me. If only I could draw, I'd draw it for you.

Please. *How can the universe be older than some of its stars?* Somebody screwed up. *Will we ever conquer disease?* No. *Will the universe expand forever, or will it stop at a point and implode?* Right then, when I'm on implosions, the train hits Park Place. One more stop before school.

My brain shifts modes. I do the mental homework checklist: math, global, English. Either I've done them, or I'll do them at lunch. The train pulls into Chambers Street.

It's 7:58, most likely—I'll know by sneaking a glance at someone's watch.* My back is aching; lint has already sneaked into my interstices. I'm tired and I'm headed off to Sequential Math, where I understand roughly 50 percent of the curriculum. But at least there I've got something to do. These subway trips are going to kill me fifteen minutes at a time.

---

*I never wear a watch. They always chafe my wrists. Also, I chew on them and lose them.

PARENTAL APPROVAL

"**N**ed, have you been smoking pot?" Mom asked. I exploded with laughter. I was in the kitchen, clipping my nails, eating cereal, and watching TV.

"What?! What makes you think that?" I turned to Mom. I had never smoked anything in my life, not even cigarettes, and I was tired of her paranoia.

"When you do homework, you turn off the overhead light and use your desk lamp. When you watch TV, you always keep the lights off. People who smoke marijuana become sensitive to light, you know."

I laughed. "Mom, when I do homework, I use my desk light because it's more *focused*. And I watch TV in the dark because there's no glare that way . . . seriously."

"*Oookay,* I'm just checking."

I'm not sure why my mother is so fixated on me and drugs. I guess it's just baseline suspicion—I'm fourteen, I'm in high school, and America is a morally repugnant cesspool of sex and substances anyway, right?

Mom and I had that little conference on a Thursday night in February. The following Saturday, I told her I had to go to the West End at 8:00 P.M. to see a band called Shrivel. Shrivel's lead guitarist, Josh, went to my school. He reportedly had a really good group, and a lot of my friends were going to see him. Mom refused to let me go. I asked her why.

"Well, because I don't know any of your friends, and I don't know what kind of people they are," she said.

Of course Mom didn't know my friends—I never brought them to the apartment. It was a three-ring circus, with her obsessing over crosswords, Dad ranting about how dirty everything was, and Daniel and Nora fighting. The people I brought over tended not to return. I *told* my mother about my friends, but those conversations always went badly:

"Mom, I met this cool kid named Sam* in school."

"Oh, yeah? What's he like?"

"He's a video game addict. He plays this game Warcraft all the time. He's up till three every night playing it."

"Sounds nice."

"He's the number five ranked Warcraft player in the *world*, Mom."

"Uh-huh. Where did he go to school?"

---

*Actually, Sam went kind of crazy as time went by. He got to the point where he played video games instead of going to school, and I'm not sure if he graduated. Hope he's doing well.

Mom always asked that—where had my friends gone to school before they came to Stuyvesant? I never had a clue; I didn't see why it was important.

So because I never brought my friends home and didn't know what junior highs they'd attended, my mother decided they were bad influences. We had a loud, drawn-out argument about the Shrivel show. In the end, we reached a compromise: Mom would let me go if Dad drove me there and back.

Dad was happy to do it—he liked any excuse to get out of the apartment. He planned to drop me off at the show at 8:00, hang out in some book-stores for a while, and pick me up at 9:30. Now, Dad isn't an embarrassing guy, but the Shrivel show was an important social gathering, and I didn't want him escorting me to and from it. I explained this to him. He understood. He dropped me off a block away from the West End and let me walk there my-self.

When I arrived, I didn't know what to do. I'd never been out to see a band before, but I had this vague idea that bands played in "clubs" or "bars," and this didn't look like either: it looked like a restaurant. Unprepared as usual, I hung around for ten minutes until my socially savvy friends, who had seen a lot of bands, showed up. They led me into the West End, through the restaurant, and down a flight of concrete stairs. Josh stood at the bottom by the basement door, asking everyone for five bucks.

Next to him was his *mother*.

"Hi!" she gushed. "Thanks so much for coming to the show! And you are . . ."

"Uh, Ned."

"Oh, Josh has told me about you. You're from Stuyvesant, right?"

"Yeah."

She kept talking, but I was no longer listening. I was pondering the inherent wrongness of the situation. A rock concert should be counterculture and youth-driven—not something you invite your *mother* to.* Rock is the opposite of mothers. Nevertheless, I paid my five dollars and walked through the door, into the West End's dim basement.

The opening band was Army of Clones. The band members were about thirteen years old, and they were terrible. The drummer seemed to be witnessing a drum set for the first time; he eyed it strangely and hit it occasionally. I don't think the bassist was even playing anything. Army of Clones had no good original songs because, at thirteen, they had no life experience.** In four years, they might be decent.

---

*Except, of course, for those mothers in "Highway to Hell" (pages 22–30). They were cool.

**Whereas Ike and I had a *lot* of life experience when we formed Wormwhole (pages 31–35). I'm telling you, we were a killer band.

I looked around at the audience. The basement was half full, with a bunch of the bands' friends milling around, chatting. But in one corner, there were . . . *adults*. Dressed in blazers and ties, sitting with perfect posture and sipping distinguished-looking drinks, they contrasted sharply with the younger members of the crowd. I saw Josh's mother among them, and then it hit me—these were the bands' *parents!* And *grand*parents! With *video cameras* to tape the gig!

On the faces of these well-off Upper West Siders, I saw the same proud "Look at my kid" grins that parents wear when they see school plays. I could just picture these people lounging at home, beaming at their videotape of Jimmy's First Gig. "Look at him sing about his teenage angst. Isn't that wonderful!"

Army of Clones finished, and two or three kids clapped. The parents stayed, recording everything, as Shrivel took the stage. The band had technical problems. The vocalist's mike went dead; no one could hear what he was screaming about. The bass amp was busted, too; at one point, the bassist stopped plucking to tie his shoes and nobody noticed. That was all right. The music was standard, whiny fare, but at least it was loud. The first song they played was the theme from *Batman*. That was good enough for me.

By now, the kids had formed a mosh pit.* Not a hardcore one, with people actually getting bloodied—just a "mini pit" where misunderstood students could vent themselves.

I never dance—I hate dancing—but I figured I could mosh a little. Anyone can mosh: just jump in and flail your arms around, right? Well, it isn't that simple. You have to know when to *start* moshing. If you start too early, you have no one to slam into and you look like an idiot. If you start too late, people give you dirty looks and call you a poser. It's a delicate balance. At the Shrivel show, I started when three or four people were going at it, and I still felt dumb. The adults didn't venture into the pit, but I'm sure it made interesting fodder for their VCRs.

As I was moshing, I noticed a girl I couldn't quite place. Then I remembered—summer camp. I'd completely forgotten her name. What was I supposed to say to her? I already have a problem with seeing people from camp in the city; it feels odd. I have an even bigger problem with, um, girls. Midway through Shrivel's set, she came up to me.

"Don't I know you from somewhere?" she asked.

"Camp."

---

*A circular area where you were supposed to jump in and smash into other people in time to the music.

"Oh, yeah." She walked away. Phew. I escaped that confrontation with monosyllabic simplicity.

The second-to-last song was hard and fast. I jumped in the pit, and some kid punched me in the chin, so I swung on ceiling pipes and kicked people in the head.

By 9:45 it was over. Shrivel left the stage; their parents packed up the cameras. Ears ringing, I climbed out of the West End and into the winter night. There, on the corner, looking at a thick history book he'd picked up from a used bookstore, was my dad. I walked up to him.

"So, Ned, how was it?" He smiled. "Oh, wait, should I talk to you? I'm not embarrassing you too much, am I? Maybe I should move away so your friends don't see me."

He has a comforting bass voice, my dad. I started laughing as we walked to the van.

HORRIBLE MENTION

Late spring, when I was fifteen, I was given a Scholastic Writing Award for a short story I wrote. Actually, it wasn't a real award—it was an honorable mention. I'm always getting honorable mentions; I used to think it was me, but now I realize that the teen world itself is full of second prizes. Nobody wants to hurt our self-esteem.

Anyway, I'd written this story earlier freshman year. Called "The Bagel Man," it was about a kid who goes to school, eats a bagel, meets an old man, and realizes the old man is freer than he is. My English teacher liked it, so I sent it off to the competition. Two months later I got the letter: "We are pleased to announce . . ."* At first I was excited, until I saw that about six hundred kids had entered the contest and three hundred won something.

The letter invited me to a ceremony on May 19. From 1:00 to 2:00 P.M. a reception would be held. From 2:00 to 3:00 P.M. the awards would be handed out. My invitation said that I could bring a guest; I

---

* The congratulatory letter was printed on the cheapest paper I'd ever seen. It looked like wax paper stolen from a deli. Have to give credit where it's due, though: I put that letter on my wall years ago, and it shows no signs of decay.

considered taking Dad but, as a fledgling teenager who wanted nothing to do with his parents, I decided against it. Dad was kind enough, however, to drive me into Manhattan.

We got stuck in traffic,* in disgusting New York City heat. Even worse, when we left our apartment in Park Slope, a group of kids on skateboards was behind us. As we came to a complete stop around Flatbush and Atlantic, they passed us by and coasted into the distance. I hate it when kids on skateboards pass me; they're already cooler than me—they have to be faster, too?

Dad dropped me off at the Fashion Institute of Technology, a college in Manhattan, at 1:50. Not bad, considering I had planned to get there at 1:00, and my family is usually *two* hours late. I got out of the van, wished Dad a safe trip home, and followed the signs for "Scholastic Writing Winners." I found myself at the entrance to the Marvin Feldman Auditorium, where a giggly blond woman asked me what my name was.

"Ned Vizzini," I told her. Not Viccini, or Zizzini, or Zazooni.** I hate my name sometimes.

"Okay, Ned," she giggled. She gave me this

---

* Dad got frustrated with the traffic, at one point leaning out his window and screaming, "MY lane! *MINE!*" at an offensive motorist. He's going to get himself killed one day.

** All of these are actual names I've been called at some point. "Viccini" used to be on the doorbell of my family's apartment.

computer-personalized name tag and a yellow index card that read:

Ned Vizzini
Stuyvesant High School
Honorable Mention
Short Short Story

I wondered what the card was for.

"Ned? Just go right up those stairs to the reception," said the woman.

I went.

Now, I didn't know that this awards ceremony was a dress-code occasion. After all, I was only getting honorable mention, and my story wasn't very good. Besides, I figured the place would be full of artistic types, and you never know what they're going to wear. So I dressed, you know . . . casually. I had on a plain white T-shirt and blue plaid shorts. *Everybody else* was in a dress or blazer, or at least a button-down shirt and tie.

I sighed, slunk over to the refreshments table, and got some punch. I was sipping it casually, elbow cocked up, when it spilled spectacularly all over my shirt and shorts. And it wasn't even that pale yellow adult-looking punch—it was bright red, like Kool-Aid.

Wiping myself off, I went from the reception

room to the auditorium, where I was shown to my seat among the other winners in the short short story category.* I was placed right in the middle of the row, so everyone could look at my huge red stain as I walked to my seat. On my left sat a glasses-clad, curly-haired boy dressed in a blazer and tie. He looked about two years younger than me. His name tag said, "Brian." To my right was an even younger blond-haired girl—I never did get her name—wearing a pristine dress. She kept leaning across me and whispering, "Kimberly, Kimberly! What'd you win?"

I turned to Brian, "So what happens now? We just get our certificates, right?"

"Nah, they have to make speeches first." He had a really deep voice, deeper than mine. "Maybe," I thought, "he's older than me and just short."

"What are these things for?" I asked, showing him my yellow index card.

"When you go up to get your award, you give your card to the guy, who reads off what's on it. Then everybody claps, and you get your award, and you sit down." I looked at Brian's index card. He'd won honorable mention, too.

The speeches began. The first lady was young

---

* "Short Short Story" is a category the literary people thought up. It means a really short story, like eight hundred words.

and unprepared. She kept saying "um" and "well" and "in fact." Most of her speech was about how lots of famous writers—the only one I remember was Bernard Malamud—had won Scholastic Writing Awards* when they were kids. And she said something about how we were the light of the future. The second speaker, an older woman, was articulate and confident. She also said we were the light of the future. The third speaker kept it brief and remarked on how imposing it was to have all these future writers in the room. And we were the light of the future.

Then the handing out of the awards began. The kids were called by category (dramatic script, science fiction, etc.); they got out of their seats and formed a line leading to the foot of the stage. From there they walked up one by one and handed their index cards to "the guy," who read off their names. Then people applauded. Just like Brian said.

Naturally, the short short story category was the last to receive awards. That gave me a chance to sit in my punch for the longest possible time. When the announcer finally called us, the girl next to me giggled and whispered, "Kimberly, I'm *sooo* nervous." We lined up single file. I was between Brian and the

---

* Incidentally, if you want to enter one of these Scholastic Writing things (who knows, you could end up winning honorable mention and spilling punch on yourself), visit this site on the Web: www.scholastic.com/artandwriting/howenter.asp. Or write to: Alliance for Young Artists & Writers, The Scholastic Art & Writing Awards, 557 Broadway, New York, NY 10012.

Kimberly girl. We walked onstage to receive our awards. I handed my index card to the guy; of course, he needed help with pronunciation.

"Vi-ZENE-ee," I told him. He read it off, and everybody clapped halfheartedly.

As they applauded, I peered down at my peers, in their suits and prim dresses. Suddenly I felt superior. It was a wonderful, virile, teenage sort of superiority. There I was, receiving an award for something I'd done completely on a whim; these kids' parents had probably forced them into the Scholastic Writing contest to earn points for Harvard.* The stain on my shirt was all part of it. It was a *statement*.

I walked back to my seat thinking about happiness. I decided that you didn't really need money, power, success, religion, a spouse, or kids to be happy. All you really needed was to feel superior. I could be a homeless druggie; I'd still be able to look at businesspeople trudging off to work and think "Hah!" because I'd be freer than them.

I thought about that for a little while. Then I decided it was all pretty stupid and, award in hand, I took the subway home.

---

* Of course, two and a half years later I'd be showing my own work to the Harvard people, begging for admission and getting soundly rejected. But that's another story (pages 186–197).

MOXY MUSIC

My dominant nerd brain was telling me to stay home and cram. My subordinate cool brain was causing problems.

It was the night before my Biology Achievement exam. Doing well on it would improve my life greatly, my nerd brain reminded me. I had to take three Achievements to attend a Good College; if I got the biology one over with at the end of freshman year, I'd have less work come crunch time. But that night my favorite band, Moxy Früvous,* was playing so my cool brain ordered me to screw the test, screw authority, be different, and go see them.

Moxy Früvous is a folk band. They use a little feedback and curse at their shows, but they are not alternative and they are not hardcore. They play accordions and sing about gambling in Canada. They have songs called "Bittersweet" and "Fly." They rely on harmony, not volume; they don't bust up their vocal cords during a set; and you'll never find them on commercial radio stations. If you want to make fun of me for liking some nerd folk band, feel free.

---

*Yes, that was their real name. As of this writing they are no longer active, but they were great.

I lay my head down on my open study guide and thought about the first time I'd seen Moxy Früvous, three months earlier, in March. It was the first time I'd ever seen a live band (Shrivel* didn't count). I begged Mom to let me go, and as usual, she would allow it only if Dad played escort.

So we got in the van and drove to the venue, a small organic place in Manhattan called the Wetlands. We arrived at 10:50; I thought Dad would leave to hang out at a bookstore or something, but he stayed—he wanted to see the band.

"Where are we going to stand?" he asked as we paid our money at the door. "I mean, I know you don't want to be seen with me, and I definitely don't want to be seen with you."

"I'll stay by that column," I said as we strode inside. "I guess you can go by the bar."

"Fine by me," Dad said. "Enjoy the concert." We shook hands and moved to separate parts of the Wetlands.

I waited for thirty minutes, breathing smoke, eavesdropping on conversations, wondering where the band was. Finally Mike, Jian, Dave, and Murray appeared on the tiny stage. The Wetlands could hold about one hundred and fifty people. That night, it was packed; everyone howled as the band emerged.

---

*Shrivel is in "Parental Approval" (pages 52–58).

They looked dangerously dorky. Jian wore a shiny purple vest; Mike, a shirt covered with multicolored Pac-Men; Dave, a black turtleneck. For the opening number, Jian got behind the drum set, Murray picked up his bass, Mike grabbed an acoustic guitar, and Dave strapped on an accordion.

Then Jian announced that there would be no music tonight—just talk. "Talk radio's getting big in America—you'd be an idiot to play music!" he said. He did a drumroll, and the band started in.

Because they use so many instruments in the studio, I had low expectations of Moxy live. Congas, bongos, accordions, pianos, organs, harmonicas— I couldn't see how the band could play all of them on-stage. But they pulled it off, substituting guitar solos for piano solos and strapping on extra in- struments when necessary. Then they started in with their bizarre stage antics. Mike dressed up as Spider-Man and shot a cap gun at the Wetlands' disco ball, proclaiming, "That rotating disco ball up there saps and saps all the strength from Spider- Man!" Dave put on a fez, declaring that he was the king of Spain.

I looked over at Dad a few times as the show pro- gressed. He kept his hat pulled low and his eyes closed, and tapped along with the music. True to his word, he ignored me completely.

Moxy played some favorites: "Video Bargainville," an accordion-driven tale of everyday life in a video store, and "King of Spain," the riches-to-rags story of a modern-day monarch. There was new material, too: the anti-employer anthem, "I Love My Boss," and "The Greatest Man in America," a song about Rush Limbaugh.

All of this led to a shattering eight-minute medley, featuring snippets of old favorites like "Love Potion Number Nine" and "Stayin' Alive," and a farcical version of "You Oughta Know." The medley ended with Dave's guitar solo; I heard someone clapping very loudly over the feedback. I peered at Dad, who always cupped his hands to produce incredibly loud applause.

Moxy left the stage, but the crowd began screaming and the guys reappeared, playing two encores. Dad and I didn't get out of the Wetlands until 1:30.

"Well, thank you," Dad said as we got into the van. "I'm pretty sure that on the entire island of Manhattan, that was the best music being played tonight."

"Yeah, they're pretty good, aren't they?" I said sheepishly. I got in the passenger seat and fell asleep. The next day, I was wide awake and brimming with energy at school.

Now here I was, three months later—with my head between the pages of my study guide. I had the chance to see Moxy again, but there was a vital test the next morning. A classic dilemma. My nerd brain told me that concerts were never that great, that I was romanticizing the one I'd seen before, that I'd better lift my face and refocus on those questions because what if I was tested on this *particular part* of the book? My cool brain told me I'd been preparing for the test for weeks, that one more night of studying wouldn't make any difference, and I'd better stop takin' orders from society.

"Mom!" I called. She came quickly to my room; Mom was especially attentive when I was studying.

"Are you okay? Do you need any tea?" she asked.

"Actually, I was wondering if I could, ah, go to this concert tonight. It's Moxy Früvous, those people I saw with Dad a couple months ago."

"Out of the question."

"What? Why?"

"Ned, it's *six o'clock*. You couldn't have planned this sooner? You have a test tomorrow; you can't be seeing *bands*."

"What if Dad came? Like he did before?"

"I know this may surprise you, but sometimes your father has better things to do than drive you around at all hours of the day and night—"

"I'll take him!" Dad shouted from the other room. "They're a great band! I'll take him!"

"Jim, don't interfere!" Mom yelled. "He has a *test* tomorrow!"

Dad and Mom continued the discussion. I closed the door to my room and went back to my study guide. My cool brain was ranting, "You could sneak out the window, Ned! Sneak out the window, dude! Be the man for once!" My nerd brain just laughed. I pulled up my chair and refocused my eyes on the page. I might not be doing the right thing, but I was doing the dorky thing—the only thing I was good at. Moxy Früvous would have approved.

POSTMARK: BLANCHEVILLE

Blancheville is a small turd of a town on the Connecticut River. The only reason I know is because it houses my summer sleep-away camp, CCRC, short for the Christian Camp and Recreation Center.* I've been coming here for five years, because my parents deem it necessary and because I have nothing to do in the city. If I were home, I'd be pacing through heat waves, eating Oreos, and playing Mega Man III.**

CCRC is coed; its campers are split into age groups called sections. Now that I'm fifteen, I'm in Explorer Village, the most independent section. I live in a platform tent with five other guys. It's a dank, smelly hole of a place—wet socks and mildewed towels strewn everywhere, a garbage can overflowing with candy wrappers . . . the green-fabric ceiling keeps the rain out and the odors in.

---

* The "Christian" part was dubious; CCRC had a short optional chapel service once a week. But that was good enough for Mom, who didn't want me missing any church over the summer.

** One of the better video games of all time.

I cook my meals over a campfire, which is intensely gratifying. Sure, the food tastes like ash, but I get to chop firewood.* And camp cuisine is a welcome departure from my New York diet of orange Hostess cupcakes and Trix cereal.

Most of my stay at Explorer Village is spent in "Festivals" and "Free Time." Festivals are the typical camp activities—hiking, swimming, soccer, Ping-Pong, fish-punching,** and general lounging. This year, it's rained almost every day, which means lots of Ping-Pong and lounging. I hate both.

But I hate Free Time more. During winter, as I trudge through school, all I want is a little time for myself. At camp, I finally get it—and it bites. What can I do with an hour in the woods of Connecticut? Read? Write? Practice my hopelessly flawed basketball shot? My campmates go "chilling," which means sitting on a rock and having light, hip conversations with girls. I could never handle light, hip conversations. (Girl: "Did you see *Heathers*?"*** Me: "Uh, nope . . . did you see, ah, *Jurassic Park*?" Girl: "No.") I spend most Free Times brooding in my tent, which has led to some Deep Realizations About Camp.

* Seriously, I love chopping wood. I wish there were somewhere to do it in New York City, like a wood-chopping gym. I'd definitely get a membership in a wood-chopping gym.

** You lean off a dock and try to punch fish in a lake, okay? It's not as fun as it sounds because the fish are too fast.

*** Cool movie about mean teenagers.

First off, it's a Darwinian popularity contest. At all times, the question on everyone's mind is, "Who's coolest?" People complain about high school cliques, but cliques at camp form more rapidly and are twice as vicious. Last year, some guys in my section set up a full-on monarchy, complete with lords and vassals. This kid Corey was a vassal; he would kneel before the lords and fetch things for them.

It's not even the lords-and-vassals thing that gets to me. It's when I'm walking and talking with X, and he runs ahead to whisper with Y and Z, and they all laugh. Bam—I'm left to wonder what I'm missing out on.

The easiest and most preferable way to be cool at camp (and everywhere, I guess) is to get with a member of the opposite sex. Even the dorky, buck-toothed guys become instantly popular when they land a fifteen-year-old girl. This is where my problems start.

I can't go up to a girl and ask her out. (Of course, "going out with" someone at CCRC is stupid because there's nowhere to go. It just means you and your counterpart hold hands and engage in some public displays of affection.) Fear of rejection isn't the only thing that holds me back—a powerful sensation of disgust does, too, as if I were in third grade and girls were icky. If I were gay, that would clear things up, but I'm not. Just inept.

This year, I had a chance—I really did—with this punk girl named Kat. She came up to me on that first day of camp and started chatting:

"Hey, Ned! Are you still reading all those Orwell books?"

"Oh, hi. Yeah. I brought some with me, actually."

"Did you bring your Devo CD?"*

"Uh, no, left it at home."

"Oh, you don't like them now? You've moved on?"

"Yeah, I like this band called Moxy—"

"I can't believe you didn't bring Devo. I realized, the way you dance to that, you would make the perfect Rude Boy!"**

For the next few days, we talked. It was classic: I liked Kat, I thought she liked me, but neither of us was forward enough to do anything. One day, this guy named Neal asked me what the deal was between me and Kat.

"Nothing, we're just friends," I answered.

Neal got with Kat frighteningly quick, forming a relationship that lasted all through camp. I was thankful; it gave me an excuse not to ask her out, which I had feared more than anything.

---

* Oh, Devo. What can I say? The nerdiest band of all time, and one of the best.

** I didn't know what a Rude Boy was either. Kat was always using punk terms I didn't know; I just nodded and smiled.

I might have had some hope with Kat if there hadn't been any dances. I can't describe how much I hate dances. Ever since fifth grade, when that girl Rebecca told me I danced like a cricket, I've been a professional wallflower. I like it, in a perverse way. Standing by the wall, surrounded by other nerdy non-dancers, a sort of camaraderie forms. It's safe there, much safer than on the floor.

As luck would have it, dances are held at CCRC every Saturday, in the rec hall. During the first dance, I sat on a Ping-Pong table by a wall for three hours. Kat grabbed me and threw me onto the floor, urging, "Come on, Ned, dance!" I walked back to my table.

I missed the second dance because I was on a canoe trip. During the third dance, they played "Whip It" so I was obliged to get up and groove with Devo. When the song ended, I went back to my tent and slept. Sleep also freed me from the final dance, and as I lay in my dirty sheets, I wondered, "What happens to the wallflowers of the world? Do they ever get laid? Do they ever get married?"

I shouldn't dwell on unpleasant subjects. Some big things happened at camp, most of them on the canoe trip—eleven campers, two counselors, five days, seventy miles. I learned a lot about myself on that trip, namely how to (A) smoke a cigarette* and (B) get high.

(A) took place the first day of the trip, after we had reached our campsite. A group of boys trekked into the woods, bringing me along. They all lit up Camels, enveloping me in a smell familiar from my high school. I was offered one and shown the proper puffing technique. I took a drag.

It was just as I'd expected from riding in unventilated yellow cabs and car-service sedans—sort of like sticking your head in a campfire and inhaling deeply. The smoke went to the back of my mouth, then lower into my throat somewhere. It was acrid, abrasive, like swallowing sand. It tasted raunchy. I got very dizzy and began hacking, and then I gave the Camel to someone else. I sat down for a while, and the aftertaste was kind of good. But not good enough to shell out three bucks a pack.

(B) took place the next night, when my friend X produced a bong and brought me down to the riverbank with Y. X told me that nothing would happen to me because smoking marijuana only affected you the third or fourth time you tried it. He passed the bong

---

*I knew I'd smoke a cigarette sooner or later. I also knew it would be overrated. I did it to get it over with, to check off another little box in my head. Now I know that when teenage boys make a pilgrimage to the woods, they're going to smoke—so I'm not missing anything if they leave me behind.

around; I don't know how much I smoked. We finished and X asked me:

"So, feeling any adverse effects?"

"No, I feel normal."

"See, I told you nothing would happen."

He turned to Y and began chatting with him. Then I started laughing. At X and Y's conversation. At anything and everything. They told me to shut up.

While I was laughing, a deep, analytical part of my brain was mumbling, "So this is what it's like to be stoned." It was like waking up at 2:00 A.M. with a 103-degree fever and stumbling through the hall to pee. I tripped over grass clumps as I went back to my tent to sleep.

The next day, I felt guilty. All those public service announcements I'd seen as a kid (in between Nintendo games) were haunting me. I justified myself the same way I'd done with the cigarette—if I hadn't smoked, I'd always be wondering if it were some great experience. Doing it, laughing a lot, getting told to shut up, and then going to sleep took a lot of the romance away.

Yet, for most of camp I haven't been stoned, or sitting through dances, or being called a "Rude Boy." I've just been trundling along, writing, practicing my bass guitar, idly picking apart leaves. Last Sunday, at our weekly Sharing Circle meeting,* the counselors and campers sat around a campfire, talking about what we'd learned from CCRC.

"Ned," one of them called, "what have you learned from camp?"

Geez. I learned that teenagers are vile creatures who grasp and exploit in the name of popularity. I learned some new songs on my bass guitar. I learned (A) and (B). I learned that hanging out is highly over-rated. I learned that I don't like Free Time. I stalled.

"Um, uh, what did I learn? Uh, let's see . . . well . . ."

"Okay, I understand. You don't get it, right?"

"Uh . . ."

The counselor smiled. "You probably think that this whole thing is stupid, right?"

"A little," I said.

"Well, someday you'll get it. Someday you'll real-ize how great camp is."

Okay. I hope so.

---

*This was a strange scene, a kind of camp love-in. At one point, the counselors asked, "Who didn't make a new friend this year? Raise your hand." One girl raised her hand and said she had made no new friends, and she hated the place. I should've gone out with her.

SOPHOMORE
YEAR

CABLE ACCESS SAYS NO

A cheerful voice answered the phone. "Long Island University. Media department. This is Mike speaking."

"Hey, Mike," I greeted in my business voice.* "I have this movie I want to put on cable access TV."

His voice became cold and critical. "Are you a *student* here?"

"A student where?"

"At LIU."

Of course, LIU. I felt stupid.

"Well, no, but I am a student. High school." I had learned to always mention that I was a student. Milk it for what it was worth.

"Uh-huh." Mike sounded like he was writing something down. "What's your movie about?"

"It's about this killer turtle that eats people. I've seen other movies on cable access, and it's on the same, you know, *level*."

"Well, come down to the studio on Monday, and we'll have a viewing, okay?" A disclosure of directions

---

*I have a great business voice. In every band I've played in, I've been the guy who makes all the phone calls because of my business voice.

followed. I wrote them on the back of my hand in green marker.

Attack of the Killer Turtle is a thirteen-minute film about life, love, and preteen girls getting eaten by a giant rabid reptile. I had filmed it over the summer with my cousin Sam. We were both fifteen and visiting our grandmothers in Massachusetts. We were bored. Sam had a video camera and a pet turtle.

We assembled some friends and shot the film in three days. Budget: zero dollars. For months afterward, *Turtle* lay dormant in one of my drawers. I showed it to my immediate family and friends but never hoped it would achieve greatness—not until I started watching Brooklyn Cable Access Television.

BCAT has three main types of programming: simulcasts of college radio stations, leftist political rantings, and fanatical religious shows. I got addicted very fast. After school, I'd slump on the couch and watch *The Fine Arts Show* (a showcase for Navajo artifacts), followed by Penelope Pitstop's* radio hour.

Being a diligent, community-minded youth, I decided to see if I could get *Attack of the Killer Turtle* on BCAT. The closed-circuit LIU station seemed like a good place to start. So the Monday after talking to Mike, I stuffed my VHS tape in my ratty coat and

---

*I don't know why Penelope didn't become a national sensation. She was a rock DJ with a super-sexy voice who talked about which celebrities got her hot. All the callers were male.

headed to the university, convincing James to come along.

James, a tall guy with glasses, has been my friend for a while. I envy him; he's one of those naturally cool, quiet people with built-in mystique. If you say, "Hey man, how's it going?" he'll wait five seconds before answering, "Fine." If you start a conversation that doesn't interest him, he'll be silent for a half hour. Plus he has a trench coat. Whenever we're together, he's the chill guy hovering in the background; I'm the manic nut talking a mile a minute.

James and I caught a number sixty-seven bus and sat in the back among the roaches. We discussed (well, mostly I discussed and James nodded) how roaches get on buses. Do they migrate at bus terminals? Enter via grungy passengers?

The sixty-seven stopped at Atlantic Avenue. We trudged past Kennedy Fried Chicken* to Long Island University. College kids were everywhere, with their slick hair, glitter makeup, and nose rings—as if I didn't see enough bodywork in high school.

James and I walked to the information desk. "Hi, I'm looking for Mike in the media department," I announced.

---

*Right. *Kennedy* Fried Chicken. For some reason, Brooklyn is full of imitation KFCs: Kennedy FC, Kansas FC—dumpy places that capitalize on the wholesome name of Kentucky Fried Chicken.

"Well," said the wrinkled, androgynous attendant, "it's near the library."

"Where's that?"

The attendant sighed and shuffled papers while it directed me. "Go left, then right down the stairs, then across the courtyard, then up the elevator, then ask somebody."

Yeah, okay. James and I quickly got lost in the maze of LIU. By trial and error, we reached the school library and questioned the librarian. "Oh, media department? In the basement." We took the elevator and entered what appeared to be a lounge: circular table, women drinking coffee, a Mac Classic on top of a file cabinet. Sitting at the coffee table was a man with very small feet, a shrunken bald head, and a puffy blue jacket. A football was the first thing that came to mind.

"Mike?"

"Yes." He shook my hand sharply.

"We're here to show you the movie," I reminded him. "Remember? I'm Ned, and this is my friend James. He, uh, helped with editing," I lied.

"Let's go see it," said Mike. He led us into an oversized closet full of VCRs, monitors, and strange black boxes. I handed him *Attack of the Killer Turtle;* he slipped it into a VCR and hit play. Unexpectedly, I filled with pride as the blank monitor flushed with color. James mumbled, Beavis-like, "This is gonna be cool."

The film opens with a slow pan of the Atlantic Ocean. A cassette recording of the Violent Femmes'* "Color Me Once" provides eerie ambiance. The camera zooms into the waves and—cut—focuses on a gargantuan turtle.

Now, offscreen, the turtle was a four-inch-long reptile that swam around in a grungy aquarium all day.** But when we shot the scene, we zoomed in on the turtle, shook the camera around, and played "x.y.u." from Smashing Pumpkins' *Mellon Collie and the Infinite Sadness****—which added up to a fairly fierce-looking beast. I glanced at Mike. He looked impressed. Cut—two girls in swimsuits on a dock. Inspired dialogue:

"What a beautiful day for a swim."

"Yeah. I have a funny feeling about this, though."

"Why? We go swimming every day."

"I just have a . . . premonition."

Nevertheless, they get in the water.

---

*A dirty folky rock band. I once saw the lead singer running through an airport, just like any other idiot trying to catch a plane.

**Sam actually loved the turtle very much and kept it well fed, but he never named it. It didn't need land like any other reptile I've ever seen; it just spent all day swimming around in its aquarium.

***A big, long rock album, the last one to be popular before hip-hop took over.

The next scene was complex to shoot. We sprinkled some turtle food in the aquarium, so the reptile would swim to the surface and nibble. We cut to the girls, screaming and flailing their arms in the water. If you squinted real hard and remembered that a bunch of bored teens were in charge, it looked like the turtle was eating the girls.

Cut—the police department (the interior of Sam's grandmother's house). Sam takes a phone call from Inspector Barzoni (me), detailing the horrific deaths of two adolescent girls at the hands of a crazed aquatic reptile.

"I'll come meet you at the docks," he says with action-movie attitude.

Cut—he jumps in a car. This scene was the most fun to film and the most stultifyingly boring to watch. We thought it would be cool to have fifteen-year-old Sam drive his grandmother's car at thirty-five miles per hour on a deserted Massachusetts road. But the scene was shot from the backseat by Sam's eleven-year-old brother, and it lasted almost five dialogue-free minutes.

"This part's too long," Mike said.

I looked over at James. He looked worried. I made the execution gesture with my finger and neck.

The film goes downhill from there. Inspector Barzoni discovers that the only way to kill the turtle is to stab it in the eyeballs with a kitchen knife, which leads to the stunning climax: Sam and I swimming around in the Atlantic Ocean, slashing at the water with rusty knives, yelling, "Die, turtle!" The turtle dies.* The tape ends.

"Well." Mike turned to us with the adult-giving-bad-news-to-kids expression. "It's good. I mean, I like what you boys are doing. But we need the original footage. We need to edit. Add sound and music. Make this look like a real movie."

"That hurts," James mouthed.

Mike handed me the cassette. "We can't edit this VHS tape," he said. "What we need is the original footage, y'know? Direct from the camera?"

"Well, maybe I can get the originals," I answered halfheartedly. There was no way I was getting the originals. I'd lost them months ago.

"The important thing," Mike said, "is that you keep in touch."

"Okay." I smiled, pretending to be reassured. It was Mike's job to reassure and my job to smile. Despite the pleasantries, I knew full well what had just happened. I had been rejected by LIU. There was no chance I was getting my movie on cable

---

*Let's clear this up, before the animal-rights people hear about it. We did *not* stab the turtle in the eyes. We jumped into Massachusetts Bay and slashed *at the water* with kitchen knives. The turtle's presence and subsequent death were sort of assumed. The only animal harmed during filming was me—I cut my foot open on a barnacle.

access—the medium that features women in purple robes ululating at all hours of the night.

As we walked out of the place, James and I decided *Attack of the Killer Turtle* was simply too groundbreaking for cable access. What we needed to do was get it on the independent film circuit. But first things first. What we *really* needed to do was eat some Kennedy Fried Chicken.*

---

*Guess what? The movie was found and is available at www.nedvizzini.com/fun/#turtle.

ROLL WITH IT

Since freshman year, I've been taking karate classes at True Power Martial Arts. I take these classes because Mom makes me. She thinks it's necessary for growing boys to have regular physical activity. I used to play soccer,* and before that, I'm sure I did some other thing.

The classes at True Power consist of stretching, punching, kicking, and performing complex self-defense techniques. I attend twice a week in the evenings. I could go in the afternoons, but the karate school has a very large window, and I'm afraid my friends will see me training as they walk home from school.

See, I hate karate. It involves physical confrontation, and physical confrontation scares the hell out of me. I'll pass a guy my age on the street and panic for no reason—clenching and unclenching my fists in my pockets and yawning to try to appear cool. Sometimes, I dream that I'm fighting people, endless

---

*When I was eight, I played in a soccer league for a season. All the other teams had cool names (Tigers, Condors), but I got stuck on a team with an insane coach named Mr. Sack, who insisted on calling us "The Sack Attack." The Sack Attack went 0–12 that season. I was the goalie.

opponents, but I punch too slowly, as if I'm underwater. It's a stupid phobia; I live with it.

Now, I'm not knocking my karate school. Jessica Green, who has been an Olympic competitor in martial arts, teaches the classes. "Sabunim" (her formal title) is constructive and patient with me, as she is with all of her students. Still, I just don't get certain things, such as "rolling my hips." In that stretching exercise, we sit on the floor, spread our legs, and lean forward—attempting to make our chests touch the ground. In every class, three or four people do this move perfectly. But my posture is so screwed up (all those hours hunched in front of the Nintendo) that I can barely get my *hands* on the floor.

"Ned, *roll* your hips," Sabunim tells me. She comes over and pushes on my back to make me stretch lower.

My "focus" is also a problem. I tend to space out in class, humming some song or fretting over tomorrow's test on cellular respiration; Sabunim has to jolt me out of deep thought.

"Ned! Are you focused?"

I nod, wiping sweat from my brow. "Yes, Sabunim." Then I tune out ASAP until the next interruption.

My uniform causes problems, too. Called a *gi*, it

harbors a deep-seated hatred for me and humiliates me whenever possible. Actually, the top part of the uniform isn't so bad. But the pants, through some loophole in physical law, manage to be too tight *and* to fall off. During jumping jacks, I have to fix them constantly, or they'll expose my boxers. Then, in response, the pants tighten up, forming a noose around my abdomen. So while everybody else is working out, I'm in a corner adjusting my clothing.

As if my own failings weren't enough, every one of my karate classes includes seven- and eight-year-old Wonderkids. They started karate when they were, like, two. They're always focused; their hips roll in directions that make me queasy. Their pants are perfectly ironed and don't fall off.

It gets better. My sister Nora is one of the Wonderkids. She's seven years younger than me, but her kicks and push-ups are better than mine—and she knows it. Thankfully, we don't attend the same class, but every Saturday, she comes home wearing her *gi* and shows me some new, sadistic contortion.

Of course, Nora and the rest of the Wonderkids are around four feet tall, which gives me a fighting advantage. And they see me as a role model—they look at how I kick during class and give me high fives. So what? When I was eight, I looked up to all fifteen-year-olds, regardless of how spastic they were. Soon all the Wonderkids will be Wonderteens, and they'll be smirking at my hip rolls like everybody else.

On Wednesday nights, we have sparring* classes. Everyone fights in rounds for an hour. There's a guy named Brendan who only comes on Wednesdays. He's about six feet two and two hundred pounds, with tree trunks for legs. Sparring with him is like taking on a swinging girder—at any time, he can just kick a leg straight out and topple me. Once or twice each Wednesday, as we rotate partners, he knocks the wind out of me. Sabunim has to rub my back until I can breathe again before she encourages me to keep fighting.

Jessica Green's True Power Martial Arts is like my high school's evil twin. Everything that I can do at Stuyvesant—concentrate, participate in class, keep my pants on—I can't manage in karate. I'm pretty anonymous at Stuy, but in karate, everyone knows my name.

Maybe the real reason that I go to karate class is because I need something to be bad at. I've always been good at school stuff: math, reading, tests, obedience. Until karate, my only problem was talking out of turn in class. Now I have something to be bad at twice a week, over and over, without hope of improvement. The humiliation is becoming addictive.

---

*Sparring means "controlled fighting." It's two people getting together and beating on each other for two minutes.

HERE COMES TROUBLE

"**A**re you a virgin?" she asked, speaking slowly and deliberately.

"Of course," I said, nodding several times. Perfectly reasonable question.

"Well, I lost my virginity . . . ah . . . the summer between ninth and tenth grades. Don't lose it too soon."

Oh, sure, that's a big problem of mine. Losing it too soon.

"How about, you know, getting to third base?* Have you ever done that?"

"Uh, no," I gulped.

"Uh-huh."

She sipped her drink. There was silence. I saw what was coming: more questions.

"So you never got laid? Have you ever felt a girl's breasts?"

After each of these, I shook my head, and she looked even more stunned.

I stopped her with a speech. "Uh, I don't think you understand. I'm a nerd. See, what we do is"—I

---

*She was considerably more graphic with her terms, but to keep things PG, I'll use the base system.

counted on my fingers—"(1) go to school, (2) get good grades, (3) come home, (4) play Magic. I'm just not good with girls."

She didn't give up. "Are your parents really over-protective or something?"

"Nope. They're great."

"And no girls like you?"

"Maybe some do. I don't talk to them much. It's probably my crooked mouth."

"Your mouth? *Noooo.* I don't think it's crooked. I think it's very sexy."

Whoa. I was talking with Amy Sohn, *New York Press* columnist, at the paper's annual "Best of Manhattan" party.* I had wanted to meet her all evening. She wrote some amazingly dirty things in a weekly newspaper read by a hundred thousand people.

I liked her. She was shorter than me, wearing something black. Stylish red glasses. Perfectly arched eyebrows. A childlike face. She reminded me of a fifth-grade teacher—not *my* fifth-grade teacher, a brown-toothed psychotic who had throttled my friend Ben** during class—but a nice, normal teacher.

"Well . . . ," she said, more casually than before, as

---

*By now I had been writing for *New York Press* for a few months, so they let me come to their catered soiree. I was the youngest writer there. I probably would have been the youngest busboy, too.

**Ben was jumping up and down saying, "I'm a froggy," and the teacher got so mad that she grabbed him and started strangling him. She was fired that day.

I sipped my cola. "If you ever do want to lose your virginity, call me. I'll loan you my *body*."*

My brain, which had churned out clever anecdotes just moments before, shut down. Was I being offered sexual favors by an older woman? Nah. Must have misheard.

"I'm sorry?" I squeaked.

"I said," she moved in close, slowly mouthing each word, "I'll loan you my body."

For a few moments, before cynicism kicked in, I was utterly thrilled. Blood rushed to my ears. I inhaled sharply.

"That's a kind offer, Amy," was all I could say.

Images raced through my mind. Lisa, last year, wearing a dark bra under a see-through shirt, licking her lips at me during class, and then telling me later she was just messing with me. Rebecca, in fifth grade, staring at me and mouthing the words, "I want a vacuum"** over and over. Girls liked to see me squirm. I guess Amy did, too.

"Don't forget," she continued. "I'll call you. We can have lunch. Or you call me."

"Okay," I said dumbly before grabbing my back-

---

*Once again, Amy was a bit more graphic, but you get the idea.

**You don't get it? Go look at yourself in a mirror and mouth those words. You'll see. . . .

pack* and running outside. The cool air cleared my mind.

She'd been joking, of course. Still, she'd told me to call her. I debated whether to do so for two days. It was nerve-racking to call a girl for anything but homework. Finally, I left a rambling message on her smarmy answering machine, asking when we could have lunch.

Later that night, while I was studying, the phone rang. It was Amy. She didn't waste time.

"Ned, about the other night—it was late, and I'd been talking to so many people, and I'd had a little too much to drink. I forget exactly what happened. Did I say I'd loan you my body?"

"Pretty much. You said that several times, actually."

"Oh, Ned, I'm so sorry. I mean, when I said it at the party you seemed calm. But your message was so nervous. I wanted to make sure your invitation for lunch was just for lunch, you know?"

"Yeah. No problem."

"I'm so sorry. Embarrassed, really."

"That's okay."

"As for lunch, I'm pretty busy now. How about we

---

*Yes, I brought my backpack to the party. I brought that backpack everywhere. I was terrified of losing it and failing high school as a result.

set aside time next Saturday to get lunch and go to a movie?"

"Sounds cool."

After I hung up, I folded my arms behind my head and smiled. It was an innocent party joke for Amy. But I got a sexual thrill, an ego-boosting apology, lunch, and a movie. For once, an adult had messed up and I had done everything right.

NO BIG DEAL

I can't bargain. I'm awful at it. And bargaining isn't just some marginally useful secondary skill. It's an important part of successful living. My friend Ike never pays the asking price for anything. My brother Daniel is the same way: he'll haggle down a candy bar. But me? My bargaining always goes like this:

Me, at some sale, cupping an overpriced object: "Uh, how much for this?"

Shifty-eyed merchant: "Five bucks."

"I'll give you three for it."

"Five bucks."

"How about three?"

"Five bucks."

"Four?"

"No."

So, it was pure lunacy for me to buy my family's Christmas presents at the local flea market. I went anyway, thinking I could improve my bargaining skills. (Besides, our family has a history of cheap, strange Christmas gifts. When I was one, Dad's big present for us was a TV—an RCA XL-100 with a busted antenna—that his friend John found on the street. It worked, but barely; the reception was so bad that Dad sprang for cable. Fourteen years later, that RCA still sat in our living room, providing us with hours of slack-jawed peace.)

On a December Sunday, I headed for the playground at P.S. 321, the public school in my neighborhood. P.S. 321 hosts a weekend flea market, where capitalism runs wild and five bucks can net you a unique and demented gift.

In the past, I hadn't bought Christmas gifts for my family because I'd been too cheap, lazy, and young. But Mom had begun complaining that she never got anything from me. ("Well, it's not that I *want* a Christmas present, Ned, but it would be *nice*.")

Pacing through the market with a pocketful of nineteen dollars and ten cents,* I found that about 60 percent of the goods were made of china—the cheap, blue-on-white Dutch kind with pictures of windmills. It was among these that I found Mom's gift: a spoon holder.

You know when you stir coffee and pull out the spoon, and it has that little droplet on its convex side? Then, when you put the spoon on your countertop, it leaves that oh-so-small circular stain? The spoon holder fixes that. It's a block of china with a spoon-

---

*By this time, I'd earned a little money from my writing, but I put it all in the bank and never touched it. So I was still cheap.

shaped depression. When you finish stirring, you rest the spoon in its place; your countertop is spared. Mom's a practical lady, dangerously practical, actually—the kind of woman who'd rather get a spoon holder than a long-stemmed rose. I was sure she'd love it. Four dollars.

Dad was next. He likes books. Big, thick books with the phrase "World Civilizations" in the title. There weren't any of those at the flea market, but I did spot a ragged 1932 edition of *The Rubaiyat*, this Persian love poem written by Omar Khayyam around the turn of the twelfth century. I had studied it in school. The book was thin, but the language was imposing. Dad would appreciate it. Seven dollars.

Next, my sister Nora. Eight years old and partial to foreign coins. I stopped to see the coin man, who displayed his wares in a leather binder. I browsed. Every coin cost more than five bucks.

"Anything cheaper?" I asked. Timidly.

The coin man—little face, big chin, long cigarette—pulled out a shoe box full of pesos, lire, shillings, and Francs and plopped it on the table.

"Twenny-five censh easch," he offered, cigarette drooping. He was trying to light up, but the wind was too strong.

I bought eight foreign coins—probably worth twenty-three cents—for two dollars. I made sure to get the ones with queens on them. Nora liked queens and was angry that U.S. coins were so male.

I had six bucks left. I was debating who to spend it on. I considered my brother Daniel,* but my present to him was not beating him up regularly. I chose to spend the money on Ike, who had introduced me to the flea market. I walked over to the army man's table.

The army man is big, with lots of skin tags. He sells patches, buttons, belts, canteens, bullets, knives, and shells. I decided to buy Ike a grenade (it wasn't a live one). The army man peddles them—spray-painted gold, complete with serial numbers—for six dollars each. I paid him, and he put the grenade in a paper bag, saying, "We don't need anybody seein' this and gettin' scared, heh, heh."

I called Ike soon as I got home. "Hey, I got you a present."

"Yeah? At the flea market?"

"Uh-huh. It's for Christmas. You want me to tell you what it is?"

"Well, if you don't, I might buy it myself."

"It's a grenade."

Silence.

"You don't like grenades?" I asked.

"Ned . . . I *love* grenades!"

---

*Daniel and I never bought presents for each other. We shared our video games, magazines, and clothes, so it was pointless to give each other stuff. Basically, anything I bought for myself was a present for him.

"Yup, I bought gifts for my whole family, too. Except my brother. But we kind of have an understanding."

"How much did you spend?"

"Nineteen bucks," I said proudly.

"Too bad, man," Ike sighed. "I could have gotten it all for ten."

BACK CAR

It's 10:30 P.M., just before Christmas, and I'm exactly where I should be—sitting in a nearly empty subway car. My bass guitar is nestled between my legs, and my Magic cards are spread out on my lap. I'm sorting the cards; it keeps my hands and mind occupied. I'm in the back car. Unless I'm going to school, I ride in the back car—because I'm guaranteed a seat and because that's where the weirdos are.

Tonight there are two. One is a husky man, sitting across from me, drinking from a bottle in a bag. He has a bald head, huge sideburns, and big square sunglasses. Standing next to him, wobbling as he clings to a strap, is a lankier guy. He's wearing a yellow headband with a big red jewel pinned to it. They're talking about Jimi Hendrix.*

"Man, you have to understand," Husky says reverently, pointing, "when Jimi was around, the electric guitar was just invented! Nobody knew what it was; nobody knew how to play it—"

"Yeah, yeah, I know," Lanky cuts in.

Husky continues, "But Jimi was a natural, see?

---

*Seminal psychedelic rock guitarist.

No schooling, nothin'. He was a natural. The sounds he made—nobody can make them anymore."

"That's the one thing I wish—that I coulda seen Jimi play," Lanky says, swinging sideways as the train takes a curve.

"You know how Jimi played?" Husky takes a swig from his bag to accentuate the question.

"How?"

Husky leans forward, almost whispering, "He played his guitar like he was doin' his mama."

I laugh. Oedipus on the number two train. I laugh so hard, my Magic cards fall from my lap and I have to pick them one by one off the brown patterned floor. The two men glare at me.

"You've got a guitar right there," Husky says, gesturing at my bass. "How are you gonna laugh? You ever heard Jimi play?"

"No." My voice cracks.

"Well, if you were doin' your mama, how would you play?"

"I'm not sure," I mumble.

"Well, there," Lanky reasons, "you're not Jimi."

I can't argue with that. The train pulls into Fourteenth Street; Husky rises and shuffles through the doors.

"Merry Christmas," he tells Lanky. He turns to me. "Yeah, and you, too."

"Thanks," I say, looking up from my cards.

Lanky seems lost without his Husky. He sits down, mumbles some more about Jimi, and hawks loogies as the tunnel lights flash by. We both have a real phlegm problem, and there's no one else in the car to stop us, so for a few stops there's this dialogue of *"Haaauck—ptooey."*

Lanky gets off at Wall Street, and stereotypical passengers get on: a college-age double date, a bearded guy trying to look smart, a frog-eyed woman eyeing him lustily. This is the back car, though— something has to happen.

At Clark Street, a foul stench enters the train, followed by a homeless man. His rotted black jacket lies in tatters on his chest. Dark stains dot his brown corduroys. He's wearing decent-looking New Balance shoes but no socks, which gives me a dead-on view of his hairy ankles. But his most striking feature is his scent. The college girls pull the tops of their shirts over their noses and giggle.

"Go back to sleep, nosy!" he yells at them. They burst out laughing.

"Hey, man," says one of the college guys, standing up. "You're stinking up this car. How about you go to another one?" The girls think he's so cool. I think his head should explode.

"Shut up, nosy!"

"Hey, look, I'll give you sixty-five cents if you go to another car. That's a lot of money."

"No, nosy!"

One of the college girls rolls a quarter across the floor—the homeless guy cocks his head as he hears it spinning on the ground. He stares at the coin as it spirals to a stop. It settles on the floor. We pull into Borough Hall. The homeless guy takes one last look at the quarter, dismisses it, and strides confidently from the train. The college kids are silent. They know he's beaten them—he didn't take their orders and he didn't take their quarter.

I grab that quarter before anyone else can. My pride's worth a lot less than twenty-five cents.

"Hey man, give me that," the college guy barks from his seat. I flip the coin to him, but I'm not a good flipper; it ends up on the floor again. "Someday some kid is going to put that quarter in his mouth," I think.

The college guy eventually picks it up and pockets it. The train pulls into Grand Army Plaza. I stow my Magic cards and sling my bass over my shoulder, to impress the college girls. One of them is nice to me. "Merry Christmas," she says.

"Yep." I zip my coat and pull my collar over my mouth. My breath moistens it, and by the time I get home, the moisture has turned to ice.

LET'S BUY BEER

I finally came home drunk. I was happy about this because Matt Groening,* in *Work Is Hell*,** lists the twenty-five steps to manhood, and "first time drunk" is number seventeen, right after "first compulsive masturbation" and just before "first car accident." I had to do it sooner or later.

It wasn't even my fault—blame it on that clerk at the Mini Mart. I stopped at the Mini Mart by my high school almost every day; this was where I bought Nacho Doritos, Original Pringles, and orange Hostess cupcakes. I bought a porno magazine there once, too, but I felt like such a loser afterward that I threw it out on the way home and never bought one again.

One Friday afternoon, I strode into the Mini Mart following a butt-numbing day at school—one of those days when, by the end of classes, I was slouching so low that my spine lay on my chair, and my eyes were level with my desk. I was with my friend Owen, who was doing his best to cheer me up.

Owen was a pudgy little bug-eyed, dark-haired,

*Creator of *The Simpsons*.

**One of his best books.

filthy-minded Russian kid who I met sophomore year. He thought of himself, in turns, as a master computer hacker, rock star, sexual savant, philosopher, skateboarder, DJ, and Gucci-wearing high-roller. You could only believe a quarter of what he said, especially if he was talking about money or girls. But he was a hell of a guy.

"Hey, Ned," he chuckled, as we entered the Mini Mart, passing the potato chips. "Let's buy beer."

My mind weighed the options. Worst-case scenario: I get busted for public drinking and start a criminal record. If you have a criminal record, you can't become a doctor. But I'd already decided against that profession.

"Okay," I said, standing by the beer fridge. "How?"

"You could probably do it with your Stuy I.D."

I'm not sure how other schools handle identification, but at Stuyvesant, we had these little white cards. Each one listed your name, your date of birth (but the year was first, and there were no slash marks—which made it very confusing), and a bar code.*

My Stuy I.D. was a plastic casualty. I'd left it in the back pocket of my jeans for two years. It had been

---

*The bar code kept track of textbooks. Whenever a teacher gave you a book, she bar-coded you "out." When you returned the book, she bar-coded you "in." If, at the end of senior year, you hadn't bar-coded in all your textbooks, you were branded a book thief and you couldn't graduate.

through the wash countless times; it was ripped in thirds and held together with Scotch tape; and it said on top, in big scripty letters, "Stuyvesant High School." There was no way that any clerk could mistake it for anything legitimate.

I showed it to Owen.

"Dude, it's cool," he said. "It just looks like it's been used a lot." At this point, we were pacing in front of the beer fridge like two stooges planning a jailbreak.

"Owen," I mumbled, pacing, "stop pacing." He stopped.

"Okay," I took a fast breath, put my hand on the metal door handle, and pulled.

It didn't budge. It was a *sliding* door. I smiled, *slid* open the door, and grabbed a Corona.

"Corona, Corona," Owen chirped, impersonating Beavis.

"Huh, yeah, Corona," I responded, as Butt-head. I do a decent Butt-head.

I proceeded to the cashier; Owen bravely stepped outside to wait for me. I put my Corona on the Lotto placemat and plopped two dollars beside it. Would two dollars pay for a twenty-two-ounce beer? I had to look as if I'd done this before.

The cashier was a scruffy Hispanic guy who sat on a stool all day watching black-and-white TV. I respect that. He turned away from the set and stared me dead in the eye. I stared back.

"I.D." He rose from his stool and held out his hand.

I reached into my pocket, tugged it out, and slapped it down in front of him, as if people were always asking for my I.D. and it was a real nuisance.

He picked it up and ran his fingers over it for a long time. Then, without warning, he took my money and rang up the sale. He put the Corona in a brown paper bag. I picked it up and left. He was already back to his TV.

Outside, Owen was fidgeting. I marched up to him.

"It worked?"

On cue, I popped the beer open with my Swiss Army knife.*

"*Aaaaaaaah, yeeeah!*" Owen actually jumped in the air and hugged me.

I drank some beer. It was like apple juice, in that it was yellow-brown and, if you drank fast enough, you didn't taste it for a few seconds. When I finally did taste it, the beer was bitter—like dirt mixed with tap water. Every gulp I took made me thirstier, until all I really wanted was a Coke. Owen and I walked to

---

*Anytime a guy gets a Swiss Army knife, he wants to use it *immediately* to pop open beers and cans of stew. Up until then, I'd only used those femmy little scissors that don't cut very well.

a more secluded street, sat on the curb, and passed the bottle back and forth until only froth remained. Then we bought another.

I had always thought alcohol was a ruse. That is, adults are never actually drunk; they just use liquor as an excuse to bump into things, have sex, and do whatever else pleases them. I assumed I'd have to put on a big show for Owen, acting stereotypically drunk. I didn't expect the beer to have any real effect on me.

The slurring began after two bottles. Light at first, then heavier as Owen and I sampled lower Manhattan's permissive Mini Marts. I knew what I wanted to say, and my mouth seemed to work fine, but the last few words of each sentence mushed together. Plus I had no volume control; I talked like someone wearing headphones.

I mentally gauged inebriation, comparing it to other forms of mental unrest, like smoking pot* and spinning around for a while in the living room. The loss of motor control and speech was interesting, but the overall effect was fatigue, and it wasn't fun to be tired.

I turned to Owen. "Okay, man, is there anywhere you want to go?"

---

* Yeah, I admit it. I smoked pot before I drank. People are always shocked about this: they don't seem to care that I smoked pot or drank—they just don't understand how I got them in the *wrong order*.

"I know a place, yeah," he said.

Owen led me uptown, through the Village, to a rundown side street—no cars but too well lit to be an alley. In the center of the street was a telephone pole, lying sideways, as if a tornado had just blown through. Circling it were punks—real, ridiculous, leather-pants-all-ripped-up, scabs-on-their-necks, skin-that's-pasty-white-where-it-isn't-filthy punks. They scared me. I stumbled behind Owen, pretending to be invisible.

Owen strode by the punks and sat down on the telephone pole. I followed. The punks—seven guys and one girl—eyed us angrily. They each had distinguishing features: an exposed nipple, a big spike sticking out somewhere, a deformed finger.

We simply sat. Nobody talked. Finally, the tallest punk, a guy with a wool hat and a dark bruise over his eye, walked up to Owen and gestured at the bottle.

"Lemme have some of that."

It was an order. Owen gave him the bottle, and the punk joined us.

"You play?" he asked Owen, indicating his guitar. Funny, I hadn't noticed that Owen had been carrying a guitar since we left school. I don't know how I missed it; it was in a big black case slung over his shoulder.

"Yeah," Owen said, unsnapping the case. "I found

this on the street a couple months ago. I think it's, like, from the sixties."

"You have an amp?"

"Yeah. A little one."

"Okay, well, my name's Aeneas."

Maybe I heard it wrong. Owen told me afterward that the guy had said, "Neevis." But I still like to think of him as Aeneas, Homeless Greek Warrior. He told us he was a runaway from Groton, Connecticut, living off Domino's Pizza "back orders."* He needed money, and he said the best way to get it was to be a street musician. Owen, Aeneas, and I trudged over to a nearby stoop and plunked down among the gum stains.

"Okay," Aeneas said. "Owen, you just play chords on the guitar. You"—he never got my name—"slap your knees to keep the beat. I'll sing."

We played.

Owen strummed E, A, B over and over while Aeneas crooned, "I got no money / It isn't funny / I need some money today / Because I run-ied away."

He was actually a good singer. Whenever someone passed by, Aeneas incorporated the person into his song: "Hey lady / Nice sweater / I need some money / If that man you're with abuses you / You

---

*A "back order" happens when somebody orders a pizza but isn't there when it's delivered. The pizza is returned to Domino's and just given away to someone who's hungry. It's an underreported act of charity.

don't have to take it / Leave him / Leave him." Whenever a remotely Hispanic-looking person approached, he belted, *No tengo el dinero / No tengo el dinero.* He sang in Spanish to a lot of Asians and black people; evidently, anyone who wasn't punk-cadaver-white was Spanish to Aeneas.

People loved us. They tossed us dimes and quarters. Whenever a really attractive woman passed by, Aeneas would walk with her for a few blocks, serenading, and return with three or four bucks. At some point, Owen turned to me and said with intensity, "You know, dude, we're really helping out the poor." I nodded.

At 8:00 P.M., it began to get dark. We stopped. Aeneas thanked us and left for a local supermarket, claiming the chicken there was easy to steal. I went home.

I entered the apartment at 9:00, right at my curfew, not considering—even for a minute—that my parents would notice I was drunk. I didn't smell, and I wasn't drooling—I just looked a little tired. I proceeded directly to the bathroom.

"Where've you been, honey?" Mom asked from the kitchen.

"With Owen," I yelled over my shoulder. "Helping the poor." I'd reached the bathroom door; it was locked. My brother was in there.

"Daniel, get out!"

"Why?"

"Because I need to take a bath!" I suddenly had this urge for a warm bath.

Mom came by, cocked her eyebrows, and said, "You were *helping the poor?*"

"Well, sort of," I smiled. "I tried my hand at being a street musician."

"*Oookay.* You're a complete lunatic, you know," Mom said, walking into her room. "But I love you, and you're home on time, which is nice. How was school?"

"Fine," I said. "I have to talk to you or Dad about applying for the Math Achievements, actually."

"Well, talk to me about it—you know your father can't handle administrative tasks."

"I protest!" Dad yelled from the living room. Was I just drunk, or were my parents unusually funny?

"Hey, Daniel!" I turned my attention to the bathroom again. "What are you doing in there?"

"Nothing! I got here *first!*" He was probably reading *Road & Track.** Because Daniel and I shared a bedroom, he always monopolized the bathroom, treating it like his private suite.

"Daniel, I need to get in there *right now!*"

---

*Daniel had taken a keen interest in cars at this point. He went to auto shows and read *Automobile, Motor Trend,* and *Car and Driver.* He still knows more about cars than anyone I know.

"Oh, calm down!" Mom shouted from her room. "What is *wrong* with you?"

"Nothing, nothing."

Finally, Daniel appeared at the door. He punched me in the arm and ran to our room. I walked into the bathroom and turned on the hot water. Climbing into the tub, I noticed I was still wearing my boxers, but I left them on.

Two minutes later, Dad entered the bathroom. I hadn't closed the shower curtain, so he saw me in the tub. In my underwear.

"Ned, Ned, Ned. Look at you."

I looked down. I did look a little silly.

"Do you want the Spanish Inquisition in here? You better start acting with a little sobriety, or your mother is going to put two and two together. Get out of this tub in ten minutes, okay? Or, if you've lost your ability to keep track of *time*, I'll cue you."

Dad left the bathroom, closing the door behind him. Then he popped his head back in. "Oh, yeah, and the obligatory father-son thing: don't come home drunk ever again."

I slid under the soapy water, smiling.

MARATHON MACHO

"You're going to run in *those?*" The white-guy lawyer pointed at my feet. He had on blue running shorts, the kind that reveal way too much, and expensive sneakers—I couldn't determine the brand. He wore a corporate-logo T-shirt that read "J & H Marsh & McLennan," with the number 3786 pinned on it.

"Yeah, I'm gonna run in these." I was wearing sandals. Big flip-floppy Tevas. About a size too large.*

"Well, good *luck,*" he snickered. He stepped away to stretch and warm up.

I was at the Chase Corporate Challenge, this thrice-annual race sponsored by Chase Manhattan Bank, which springs corporate cogs from their offices and gets them to run around Central Park for an hour. It's a 5K race, from Strawberry Fields up around the top of the park to the boathouse. There would be no official winners (or losers) except Chase, which got to publicize its healthy, caring image.

The race wasn't free; to register, you had to pay Chase twelve dollars. You then got a number and

---

*My grandmother always bought me these sandals for Christmas, always a size too large, as if anticipating future foot growth.

a company T-shirt, which you wore to "support your corporate team." That mentality prevailed at the Challenge—that we're-all-in-it-together company brotherhood that men fall back on when they have only their jobs and their TVs. I saw guys slapping each other's backs, saying, "Let's win one for Citibank," and women stretching intensely, chatting up their coworkers. A high school varsity atmosphere.

I was there because earlier that day Erin had asked me to go. I was interning in my parents' office,* carrying around computer printouts, when she approached. Red hair. Glasses. Blindingly pretty. She was far too old for me—in her late twenties—but talking to her was a thrill.

"Hey, Ned!" Erin smiled, as if just hit by a wonderful idea. "Do you want to run today?"

"Sure!" I nodded. I predicted some office thing, like the annual softball game or running around the block a few times. "Ah, *where* do I run?"

"In Central Park."

Oh, boy. "Uh, how *far* do I run?" I asked.

"Three miles."

Okay, that sounded easy enough. Erin got my

---

*My parents jointly run a family business. Every summer since I was fourteen, they've offered me a job at their office, and some years I've been so desperate for cash that I agreed to do it. That summer, I worked in research and development to get a little money. *Very* little money. I think my parents paid me less than minimum wage. Erin was some sort of midlevel manager there.

T-shirt and number (4112), and then told me where to go.

"The race starts after work, at Strawberry Fields by the Daniel Webster statue. And bring a raincoat. It's coming down hard."

"Oh, it's raining?" I stuck out my neck, peering through a nearby office window. Thick, nasty-looking drops spattered the glass. Later that night, on the Weather Channel, they'd call it a tropical storm.

Erin tilted her head. "Do you mind running in the rain?"

"No, no, ah, it's just some rain," I said, looking down, wondering why I love punishment.

Erin smiled. "You know, Ned—" Oh no, she was going to make eye contact; I could feel it. "I'm really glad you decided to do this." There it was, open-eye staring. I looked away. "I'm in charge of getting people involved in this race every year. A lot of them quit on me today because of the weather. So, thanks."

"Anytime, Erin."

I left the office at 5:00 P.M., carrying an inordinate amount of junk. First, I had the clothes: the T-shirt I was going to wear home, the *new* T-shirt with the company logo, and my jacket. Then I had an umbrella, an eighties-era Walkman, and *The Fellowship of the Ring*, a book I'd been reading on and off for two years. It never occurred to me that this stuff might impede my running ability.

When I arrived at the race, a few hundred amateur athletes were already there, their ankles propped up on park benches, stretching. I tried talking to a few, but they brushed me off; I wasn't from their *company*. I stood with my coworkers.

"So, Ned, why are you wearing sandals and socks?" one of them asked.

Everyone thought that was funny. I didn't see what was wrong with sandals and socks. I'd worn them to work because I'd lost my shoes.* "Uh, I just happened to wear 'em today. I didn't even know about the race until this afternoon."

"Where's your number?"

That was another problem. I had forgotten to ask for a pin at work, so I had no way to attach my racing number to my shirt. I figured I'd just tie it on with my extra clothes.

"You better put that number on soon. The race is starting."

I took my two T-shirts and jacket and tied them around my waist—it almost looked like an inner tube. I slid my running number under this ring of

---

*I lose my shoes a lot. They get put behind the radiator or something, and I can't find them for a few days; eventually, they show up.

clothing, put the Walkman and book in an oversized pants pocket, and stuck the umbrella in the front of my pants.

Some announcer I couldn't see was saying, "From the Chase family and from everybody who helped organize this race, we want to thank you for coming out in the rain!" People clapped. "We're ready to begin, so stay safe and have a great time! On your marks . . . get set . . . go!"

"Nonserious runners should stay to the side!" someone yelled as I started jogging. My Tevas flip-flopped all over the place, making loud smacking noises; people gave looks. The umbrella in my pants began to chafe my thigh almost immediately. For a while, the only noises I heard were the huffing of breath and slapping of sandals.

"How far are we into the race?" I asked a kindly looking gentleman after what I thought was a long time.

"Oh, a quarter mile."

"A quarter mile?!" This was going to be much harder than I thought. The Walkman in my pocket was getting heavy; it hit my leg with every stride. My pants were soaked; I used one hand to keep them from falling down.

I started walking fast instead of running. I wanted to give up and just sit down, but three things kept me going. First, those fifty-something balding guys who were in better shape than me, making better time than me. Second, those damn Nike commercials, where the big athlete at the end says, "Believe in your*self.*" They always emphasize the *self,* and I figured, hey, I can do this. And third, more than anything else, there was Erin. Was she somewhere in the race? She'd helped organize it; she must be somewhere nearby. Maybe she was waiting at the finish line, and if she was, I didn't want to look like a tired, wet, sweaty idiot. I wanted to hold my head high and be a real man.

So I kept running. When I got tired, I hawked up a loogie and smeared it all over my face, which really grossed out the other runners but kept me refreshed. Every time I got my hands on a cup of water, I poured it on my head. I stomped in every puddle. Halfway through the race, I was an orgy of spit, snot, and rainwater.

To pass time, I sang the Doors'* "L.A. Woman" as I ran. That song has the perfect runner's beat; it was in sync with my slapping sandals. I found myself belting out the lyrics as I rounded corners, "L.A. woman! / You're my woman!" I cut the volume occasionally, never sure when I'd run into Erin.

Then, suddenly, I was at the finish line. It was a

*Seminal psychedelic rock band.

sorry scene. Chase volunteer cheerleader-types patted me on the back, said "Good job," gave me *another* T-shirt, and doled out generic soda and Power
Bars. (If you can imagine a candy bar with all the
good stuff—chocolate, caramel, peanuts—replaced
by carob, you've got your Power Bar right there.)

I looked around. Erin was nowhere in sight.

I tried to convince myself that the Chase Corporate Challenge had been a good deal. I factored in the
free T-shirts, running number, water, soda, Power
Bars, and exercise, which was the best I'd received
since routinely getting beaten up at Pure Energy Martial Arts. But who was I kidding? After leaving the
park, I checked myself out in the mirror of a local
Burger King: I was a soppy teenage Frankenstein—
snot all over my face, sweat and rain mixed in the
armpits of my shirt, socks and sandals covered in
mud.

The next day, of course, Erin was at work, all
smiles. "So, Ned, how'd you do in the race?"

"Okay, I guess."

"Great, great! Did you hear how good Jack did?"

Jack was Erin's boyfriend, who also worked in the
office. I tried not to think about him.

"Come, look!" She led me over to the coffee machine, where she had posted a chart with the partic-
ipants' names and running times. The other runners

had kept track of how long they'd taken and reported to Erin. I guessed this chart was something she did every year.

"There's Jack!" She pointed. Next to his name was, "27 minutes! WOW!"

"How long did you take, Ned?" Erin asked. "So I can put you on the chart."

I had probably run for an hour. "Forty minutes," I said.

"Oh, great. Great job, and I hope you do it if you work here next summer, too." She put my name on the chart, poured herself a cup of coffee, and sipped, leaving lipstick all over the rim.

JUNIOR YEAR

MAGIC MOMENTS

Teenage boys are (1) many in number; (2) bored out of their minds. And they get tired of pornography. So, when I was twelve, a California mathematician named Richard Garfield began selling a game called Magic: The Gathering.

You remember Dungeons and Dragons, the fantasy role-playing game, where you spend hours pretending you're an elf or a dwarf on an adventure? Or Pokémon, which is a descendant of the game? Magic's like that, but it uses cards. Each player has a sixty-card deck, and each card depicts a troll, gnome, or some other Dungeons and Dragons–ish creature.* The players draw seven of these cards to make a hand; then they use this hand to attack each other, taking away life points with successful hits. Each player starts out with twenty life points; when someone hits zero, he dies. Game over.

The rules get a lot more complicated. Just know that when you win a game of Magic, you get a sharp,

---

*Many of these "creatures" are scantily clad, buxom females. In fact, some early Magic cards were banned from later editions because they were too sexually suggestive. The one I remember was Earthbind, which featured this teenage-looking elf tied down with leather straps.

semisexual thrill that makes you forget, briefly, that you're a card-obsessed loser.

I love the game, as do a lot of people—Magic is a global industry with tens of thousands of cards.*

It takes money to play Magic. The cards are sold in packs, like cigarettes, about three dollars and fifty cents for fifteen.** Those fifteen cards, however, aren't random. Just as baseball cards have "rookies" and "all-stars," Magic packs contain eleven "commons" (virtually worthless cards), three "uncommons" (might be worth a buck or two), and one "rare" (the real goodies; some have double-digit price tags). Every few months an "expansion set" is released, containing a new group of cards with dozens of fresh rares for players to collect. Each expansion set has its own name and packaging so that a Magic player making a purchase sounds like a smoker, "Yeah, I'll have a pack of 'Legacy.'" I'm down to a pack a day.

Magic also offers a chance to make money. Certain ultrarare cards are worth more than three hundred bucks, and if you get your hands on them, there's a world of collectors who will buy. Also, Magic tour-

---

*If you want to learn the rules to Magic, the Web is a good place to go. It makes sense that the greasy folk who play the game have time to put up countless Web sites about it; for starters, check out www.pojo.com/magic/.

**You can buy Magic cards at comic book shops, newsstands, and specialty gaming stores—anywhere you can get decent *Star Trek* memorabilia.

naments sponsored by the Duelists' Convocation offer cash prizes. Real cash. I know a kid who won twenty-five thousand dollars in the Magic Grand Prix in Japan.

For years, the New York Magic "scene" has been dominated by a single gaming hall: an oversized room full of tables called Neutral Ground. Occupying the entire fourth floor of 122 West Twenty-sixth Street, Neutral Ground is nerd heaven. At all hours of the day and night, you can pay seven dollars to enter the place and play Magic with people as addicted as you are.

I used to attend Neutral Ground's Friday tournaments about once a month. Fridays at the Ground were a trip. Hardcore gamers sat in stained T-shirts methodically opening packs of cards, while businessmen perused glass display cases, picking out seventy-five-dollar rares. The businessmen wore stylish coats and carried attaché cases, but as soon as they entered Neutral Ground, they were like little kids, gibbering about this and that card. The patrons ranged in age from twelve to fifty, but most were in their twenties, and everyone acted like teenagers. Occasionally, a girl would join the tournament, but the women who play Magic are a wild and woolly lot: they either look and smell like train-hopping hoboes, or they're with male Magic players, who value them more than anything on earth.

Once, I spent all night at Neutral Ground. It

wasn't hard. I told my parents I was sleeping at James's house* and went into Manhattan at 6:30 P.M. I entered the Friday tourney at 7:30 and played until 12:30 A.M. (I lost), steadily consuming a supply of Nacho Doritos and Mountain Dew. I played with Tony, a twelve-year-old whose mom let him practically live at Neutral Ground. I tried to play with Steve O'Mahoney-Schwartz—the highest ranked Magic player on the East Coast—but he spurned me. Out of my league.

Around 1:15 A.M., I started a "melee game"—a Magic game with more than two players. My opponents were a marine who kept telling the same joke about a woman in a tollbooth, a turtle-esque man half my height, and a pudgy guy who kept picking at his ear. Our game began at 1:30, and Time, in a wacky, late-night trick I hadn't seen before, jumped forward three hours. I looked down at my cards at 2:00 and glanced up to find it was 4:30.

"Gotta go, guys," I told my opponents. They were doped up on Mountain Dew by then; they smiled and patted me on the back. I gathered up my things and staggered (my thighs had fallen asleep) onto Seventh Avenue. The birds were singing. Sunrise.

---

*James was my "friend of convenience." I think a lot of teenagers have one—the friend you tell your parents you're staying with when you're really doing something illicit. James was perfect because my mom knew his mom (so there was a degree of trust) but didn't talk to her that often (so there was little chance of getting caught).

The subways didn't run so well at that hour. I had to wait twenty minutes for a train, but I got home okay. I ate breakfast at a diner at 5:45, watched the sky turn blue, and told the waitress I'd been out all night "looking for trouble." I went home around 6:45, slept for ten minutes, and got back on the train. It was Saturday morning, and I had to volunteer at my high school.*

Magic shaped up to be my adolescent pastime, the way video games were my childhood sport. I eased into conversations about it that sounded like gibberish to everyone else. ("Ball Lightning is crap! It always gets Bolted or Incinerated or Black Knight-ed!") My mind slipped into thinking about Magic like hands under a pillow.

See, at the cusp of puberty, I had to make a choice: Magic or girls. And, well, Magic was right there. You know?

---

* It was Stuyvesant Tour Day or something, when all the kids who passed "The Stuy Test" (pages 14–21) for that year got to look at the school to decide if they wanted to attend. I stood around directing parents and answering kids' questions. I had fun.

GOOFY FOOT FORWARD

I went snowboarding, which I shouldn't have done because the SATs were only five months away and I had yet to crack the big red prep book. Owen called and convinced me.

"Ned, this weekend, you have to go snowboarding with me."

"Why?"

"Because," he articulated carefully, "it is the coolest thing you will ever do."

"Uh . . ." I needed a way out. I had gone skiing once when I was eight. I remembered the ground hitting me again and again. "Owen, I can't snowboard. I can't even ski."

"So? It's easier than skiing, 'cause there's one less ski to worry about. C'mon, dude. You come snowboarding with me, you'll be the monsta mack.* You'll be the shred *master*. All the ski bunnies will flock to you."

"Ski bunnies?"

"Yeah. You know, the hot girls who hang out at ski slopes?"

---

*A favorite Owen-ism. He also said "the mackinator" a lot.

"Oh. I think I saw one in a movie once."

"Ned, they are real. I tell you, they are *real.*"

"Fine," I told Owen, "I'll go, just to try it out or whatever."

We left on New Year's Day. I woke up at 8:30 and packed enthusiastically. For some reason, I felt cool and confident about the whole trip. I wore jeans and a doofy hat, sure, but I was going *snowboarding,* like what's-his-name from the American Express ads. This was x-treme. (Well, not that x-treme—I covered trip expenses with one hundred twenty dollars from my parents.)

Owen's dad pulled up at 9:00 A.M. in a snow-colored car and loaded my stuff (one measly bag of jeans and underwear) into the trunk. I opened the car door and greeted Owen. He was decked out: shiny snowboarding pants, nice gripping gloves, face-hugging Oakley sunglasses.

"You like my gear?" he asked.

"Move over," I said and sat down.

The trip was relaxing for a weird reason: Owen's family* mainly spoke Russian. This freed me from the need to have vapid, claustrophobic car conversations with them (the ones where you talk about how school's going and which colleges you might apply

---

*Owen has the perfect nuclear family: mom, dad, brother, sister. The sister and mom seemed to be together at all times and were very quiet in the car, except when the sister was making faces or spitting at me.

to). Owen and I rehashed old episodes of *Beavis and Butt-head*.

He laid out his plans for the trip. We'd get to the Poconos by afternoon, rent our boards, get me some pants and a real hat, slide around on the hills for a few hours, and then come back to the Jacuzzi in the motel and score with whatever ski bunnies we'd picked up. I nodded at all these points. They took my mind off vomiting, which was becoming a distinct possibility as we entered our third hour on Route 80.

We reached the Montage ski resort around 1:00. The place reminded me of the city—the parking lot was full, people hurried everywhere, the ski lifts never stopped moving. Owen and I, glad to be out of the car, hopped over to the ski rental shop. It was a family business, run by two generations of scraggly guys. As soon as we entered, the spending began.

"Here, Ned—get these pants, only fifteen dollars for two days' rental. What's your shoe size? The board is thirty-five bucks a day, sixty for two days. You sure you don't want a hat?"

I rented a snowboard and some pants, each for two days, while eyeing a sign that read, "AB-SOLUTELY NO REFUNDS." I signed a form stipulating that if I got injured, it was my own fault. Right about then, the store clerk asked me, "Are you regular or goofy?"

"What?"

"Do you put your right foot forward when you snowboard, or your left?"

"Uh, I have no idea."

"Well, if you were running on ice and you had to slide to a stop, when you slid, would you put your right or left foot forward?" Luckily, Owen and I had been sliding around on ice as his dad parked, so I remembered it was my . . . left foot.

"That's goofy," said the clerk.

He went to the back of the store and returned with a size twelve goofy-footed snowboard and my special boots. I put them on and negotiated the board's buckles, which were like plastic bear traps. Finally, I managed to get both feet in and stand up. I couldn't move, though. Snowboards are made of fiberglass and weigh a good ten pounds; all I could do was jump up and down and make big *fwaping* noises.

"All right!" I slapped Owen's open palm. He had gotten on his board, too.

The next order of business was buying lift tickets. Owen explained that Montage's ski lifts were overseen by beady-eyed security freaks who checked everyone for these tiny stickers that went on your jacket. The lift tickets were advertised at thirty-three dollars, but they cost us thirty-eight because of some holiday loophole. I sighed and paid up. At last, we were ready to snowboard.

We headed for the bunny hill. Owen said I had to do the bunny hill three or four times before I could progress to higher levels like "White Lightning."

And here I learned the sick truth about snow-boarding—the *shambling*. Once you're strapped onto a snowboard, you're not going anywhere. A board doesn't let you wiggle around on level ground like skis do. So in order to get to a lift, you have to un-buckle one foot and "walk" with one leg on the snow-board and one leg off. Everyone at Montage was doing this, shuffling around like crippled grizzlies. You never see that on ESPN2.

Owen and I shambled over to the lift, waiting be-hind a legion of bad snowboarders and skiers—most of them yappy little kids. We got in our seats and rode up the bunny hill, which was forty or fifty feet high. At the top, we restrapped our feet onto our boards and managed, by sliding and crawling, to pull ourselves to the slope's edge. I stood up and looked over at Owen, ready to say something monumental like, "Here we go, dude." He was already heading downhill.

I pulled my weight over the lip of the hill and snowboarded. I don't know how this sport became associated with raucous music; I felt peaceful, pensive. There was a quiet sound of sifting snow, a soft rush of wind. I didn't even feel like I was moving fast, except when I glanced at the trees.

The problem was stopping. As I approached the bottom of the hill, I realized I had no clue how to end my ride. I knew how the pros did it—they turned their boards sideways—but that was out of the question. My board had no friction; if I turned sideways, I'd hit that many more people as I skidded along into the parking lot. I decided to fall down carefully, easing my butt into contact with the ground, like an old man getting in a bathtub. As soon as I touched snow, though, I spun out—landing facedown in front of a parked snowmobile. I pulled my board out from under me and adjusted my pants.

"Nice job!" Owen yelled. We went up again.

After two or three shots at the bunny hill, we decided to hit the next step—Montage's beginner track, "Cannonball." Cannonball was an entirely different class of slope, thirty or forty times longer than the bunny hill, with a ten-minute trip up the ski lift. Owen was happy. I knew I was going to die.

We reached the top, shook hands, agreed to a manly race, and started off. About a hundred feet down, I realized I wasn't goofy-footed. I mean, that alone would explain my board's tendency to turn right, as if gravitating toward the ski lift's metal support pillars. If I bent my back, I could sort of stay straight—but not without crossing the paths of good snowboarders, who yelled at me as they whizzed by. I was going much too fast, break-a-leg, break-a-skull fast. I went to the right side of the slope, now going slowly down Cannonball, grabbing those metal support pillars to stop myself every few seconds, but still going. Sort of.

About this time, Owen was breaking his wrist.

I kept hitting trees. People riding in the lift looked down on me and laughed. A few times, my buckles popped and I lay sopping in the snow without my board. After fifteen minutes of hacking around, I reached the bottom of Cannonball, flipping backward and slamming my head into the ground right in front of Owen's family, who'd finished skiing and were waiting so we could get lunch. They asked eagerly, in Russian, then in English:

"Where's Owen?"

"Uh, I dunno." I figured he'd already beaten me to the finish, he'd been doing so well. I turned to see him walking down the hill, holding his board under his right arm. He looked mad.

"Hey, Owen! You okay?"

"Dude, I think I broke my wrist." He held up a limp left hand.

"What?! You're kidding! I thought I was the one who was gonna get hurt."

"Yeah, me too!"

Owen showed the suspect wrist to his dad, who's a doctor. His dad simply said, "Ah. Broken."

Owen yelled profanities at the mountain and began talking to his family in Russian. I politely stood aside and looked for ski bunnies.

Owen's family took him to the local emergency room. I stayed around Montage and got more proficient on the bunny slope, but never learned how to stop. I stayed far away from Cannonball. We drove home that evening, Owen in a splint.

I was happy—I'd wanted to leave early anyway. Owen was happy—he could use his cast to impress girls. Happiest of all, though, was the older guy at the rental store, who tapped his calculator as his goods were returned a day early. Now I understood. "ABSOLUTELY NO REFUNDS."

EVERYBODY LOVES
A WHEELCHAIR

Of all the sports, it had to be volleyball. We do soft-ball, football, hockey, basketball, running, and weight training during gym, but I sprained my ankle in *volleyball*. One thing was sure: I wouldn't tell anyone it was volleyball. I'd say it was soccer—or a mugging.

The injury happened quickly. I jumped to block a spike; I was concentrating on the ball, not on my legs. As I landed, I felt my right foot turn inward. I glanced down to see the sole of my sneaker head-on. There was pain, but it was a funny pain. I laughed and hopped around on one leg.

"Young man, are you injured?" Mr. Stanley asked. Mr. Stanley, my bald gym teacher, hadn't spoken to me directly all term.

"Yup," I replied, hobbling.

"Young man, you have to go to the nurse's office. It's right across the hall."

"Okay." I bounced out on my good leg.

"Young man," Mr. Stanley said again, but this time he was talking to one of my volleyball teammates, a blond jock whose name I've forgotten. "Please help this young man to the nurse's office."

The jock held me up as I staggered out of the gym. "C'mon," he encouraged, "you can do it."

I had never actually seen the nurse's office before (I stayed pretty healthy in high school). It looked just as I expected. White walls and informative posters:

"Oh, boy. What happened to you?" the nurse's assistant asked. She was young, a student, possibly a junior like me.

"I fell in gym." I tried to chuckle.

"Well, get up on this table, and I'll get you some ice." She motioned me with her chubby hands. I did as she said, removing my right shoe and sock. My ankle didn't look too bad . . .

The assistant yelped. "Boy, is that swollen!" I looked at my left ankle for comparison; the right one was twice as big.

"Margie, come here!" the assistant called. A short African-American woman walked in with the harried, seen-it-all confidence of a high school nurse.

She took one look at my foot, then at my face. "Well, honey, you sprained your ankle good." She smiled.

"Are you sure it's sprained? Maybe it's just twisted." I had this idea that twists were better than sprains. A twist you could walk off. A sprain put you in crutches.

"Sprained, honey, sprained good," Margie said. "Look at that bird's egg." She pointed at the swelling.

"Is it broken?" I had never broken anything before.

"Probably not. You'll have to have a doctor look at it." She placed an ice pack against my foot. "Now, honey, what we need to do is call your parents."

Margie tied the ice pack to my foot as her assistant entered with a wheelchair. "Hop in," the assistant said, gesturing.

I did. I was grinning. I'd always wanted to ride in a wheelchair. The assistant wheeled me out of the room.

"I want to do it myself," I protested. I grabbed hold of the wheels and propelled my chair over to the phone, where Margie was calling my dad.

"Hello, this is the Stuyvesant High School nurse's office, calling about your son." For some reason, she wouldn't say my name. "Your son has been injured, and you need to come by to pick him up." I found out later that since school nurses aren't doctors, they're not allowed to tell parents how their children have been hurt at school. All they can say is, "Your son/daughter has been injured."

"He wants to talk to you," Margie said, handing me the phone.

"Hey, Dad. I sprained my ankle in volleyball."

Dad let out a long breath. I'd ruined his day. "Fine, I'm coming down to get you," he said. We hung up.

"Well, honey, what you need to do now is get your stuff from your gym locker." Margie grabbed my wheelchair handles and pushed me into the hall; I took it from there. It was weird—almost an out-of-body experience—to roll around Stuyvesant in a wheelchair. It put me very close to the ground and made me feel four or five years old. It reminded me of how big and snarling my peers were.

"What did you do to yourself, spaz?" someone from my Latin class asked as I rolled toward the elevator.

"Yo, man, you stole a wheelchair?" That was Owen. He'd caught a glimpse of the chair and got excited. "Whoa, awesome, who'd you jack it from? Man, this is so cool, what are you gonna do with it—oh, dude, you really hurt yourself!"

"Yeah."

"Man, I thought you just took the chair. You really hurt yourself? Did you break your leg?"

"No."

Owen ran off to tell his friends I'd broken my leg. I got in the elevator—Stuyvesant's elevators were reserved for teachers and disabled kids; I'd never been in one before. I rode up to the fifth floor and wheeled myself to the boys' locker room.*

From here, things got cartoonish. As I entered the locker room, the door closed on my wheelchair, knocking me forward, smacking my bad foot into the cement wall. Deadening bolts of pain shot up my leg. The wheelchair was fairly old, and it had a huge turning radius; I couldn't maneuver very well. So I banged my foot a couple more times before getting anywhere near my locker.

I wasn't just in pain—I was scared, rolling around in a deserted locker room. All the guys were gone: the fat ones, the hairy ones, the ones bragging about girls. It was too silent.

I got out of the wheelchair and hopped the last ten feet to my locker. I opened my lock, grabbed my backpack and my Magic cards, and hauled them over to the wheelchair, where I sat down and put my stuff

---

*For some reason, the gym was on the third floor but the locker room was on the fifth floor—ask the people who built my high school.

on my lap. Then I got out of the room as fast as possible (which wasn't very fast), because the whole scene was beginning to remind me of *Event Horizon*.*

Outside, some girls were hanging out at their school lockers in the hall—the lockers near the guys' changing room all belonged to attractive females. They glanced at me inquisitively before checking me off as someone they'd dismissed before. The wheelchair and a swollen, naked foot warranted second glances, but not thirds—and certainly not any help. I wheeled back to the nurse's office.

I needed to fill out some official papers: How did I injure myself? Where on my body? Where in the building? The point of the paperwork, I figured, was to prove that the school was in no way responsible for my falling down and that all the professionals involved had treated me properly.

I asked Margie about her experiences as a high school nurse.

"Been here twelve years," she told me.

"What's the stupidest thing you ever saw?"

Her eyes lit up. "Oh, definitely, when this girl came in holding three teeth in her hand. She'd been sliding down an escalator handrail, see, and she

---

* *Event Horizon* is the scariest movie ever made. In it a ship travels through a black hole and comes back inherently evil. Sounds stupid, but when the ship starts killing people by depressurizing them, and Sam Neill is running around with his body all cut up, and Laurence Fishburne is on fire, and people are ripping their own eyes out, believe me, it's *not* cool.

flew off the end, right into a wall. So I tell her, 'I need to call your father—what's his number?' And she says, 'I dunno.' She has no idea what her father's number is, doesn't even know where he works. I have to call some friend who calls the *uncle* who calls the father."

"Good story."

"Stupid girl. Really. They took her away, gave her some new teeth. I see her around sometimes."

Eventually, a phone rang in the nurse's office. My dad had arrived. I wheeled down to the chandelier-lit Stuyvesant lobby, kicked open the doors, and rolled across the sidewalk to the curb, where the family van awaited. Mom was in the front seat, looking distressed at my condition. Dad sat behind the wheel, wearing sunglasses against the glare.

"My goodness, honey, are you okay?" Mom leapt from the van and grabbed the back of my chair.

"Well, I've been stumbling around like an idiot for a while," I said. "And I've been blown away by the support I've received from friends . . . and from my dear father."

Dad was still sitting in the driver's seat, with his hands on the wheel.

"Jim, you're *despicable*," Mom said. "Get out here and help your son."

"*Hmmmm?* Oh, yes." Dad smiled. He was just

messing around. He got out of the van and helped me into the backseat. "How you doing, son?" he asked. "This injury might be good for you; it'll give you a chance to take a load off."

As I climbed into the van, I saw my math teacher, Mr. Pingeon, standing on the sidewalk taking a cigarette break. Apparently, he had no teachers' lounge to smoke in. He waggled his finger at me, grinning. Everybody loves a wheelchair.

THE VIEW

I have a short and brutal history with television. When I was a baby, Mom somehow got me in a diaper commercial that ran on network TV for months. I never saw it—first, I was a baby; second, no one taped it because VCRs weren't around yet (at least in my family). I never did any more diaper ads, either, because I was a "bad baby"—the kind who scream and cry like normal children, as opposed to the "good babies"* who sit still while being taped for television commercials.

Then, when I was nine or ten, Nickelodeon came to my school and taped our fourth-grade class cleaning up a local park for a segment called "The Big Help."** The idea was to show kids helping the environment. On one of the Big Help promos, I was featured in extreme close-up, screaming, *Heeeelp!* That appearance prompted calls from my cousins in Philadelphia ("Ned, you're on TV! You're on *TV!*").

My third chance came the June between junior

---

* "Good baby" and "bad baby" are actual advertising terms.

** Years later, at summer camp, I mentioned to some kid that I was on "The Big Help," and he looked at me wide-eyed. "Oh yeahhh," he said. "I remember you. They showed you for years, man! *'Heeeelp!'* But they showed you too much, man; by the end, you were overexposed."

and senior year. I was called by *The View*, a nationally syndicated talk show, where five female "personalities" sit on a couch for an hour, discussing current events and doling out advice. I was called because the producers of the show wanted me on as a guest—they had seen an article I'd written for *The New York Times Magazine*.

Okay, full story. In the spring of that year, the editor of *The New York Times Magazine*, who had seen my essays in *New York Press*, decided I would be a good person to contribute to the magazine's "Being Thirteen" issue—an in-depth survey of thirteen-year-olds in America. I was commissioned to write an advice column for a typical thirteen-year-old. I did the job. The article appeared that May, and the *Times* paid me one thousand dollars.* I thought that was the end of it. But then Ronnie, this guy from *The View*, called and asked if I was interested in being a guest on the show. He offered me two front-row seats at a live broadcast to see what it was like.

I flipped. I'd always wanted to be on TV—real TV, not diaper commercials or "Big Help" ads—for all the typical reasons. Doesn't everybody want to be on TV for the same stupid reasons? Fame, money, anonymous adoration that somehow fixes all your prob-

*Getting my money was quite a task. The *Times* simply forgot to pay me. I had to keep calling and calling until they sent over my check; they said they had "accounting problems."

lems? Enough of writing silly little articles, dude—I was ready for the Big Time.

There was just one problem. Ronnie was giving me two tickets.* I'd learned that any time adults give you two tickets to anything, they expect you to bring a girl, and I didn't have a girl to bring. Not even a prospect. I could always bring some guy friend, but then the *View* people might think I was gay and book me as "gay teen voice, Ned Vizzini." I didn't want to misrepresent the gay community.

So I convinced Ronnie to give me four tickets; that way, I could show up with three buddies, like the typical, normal, heterosexual male I was trying to become. With the tickets clinched, I started making phone calls.

First, I phoned Hector, my drummer friend. I played in two bands in high school (neither was as good as Wormwhole),** and Hector drummed in both of them. He looked like a drummer: short, dirty, with a huge forehead. He walked like a caveman, and he was brutally honest and loyal.

"Hey, Hector, you wanna crash a TV show?" I tried to sound cool.

"Oh, wow! Yeah! Sure! What show?"

---

*I always wonder about this on game shows. When someone wins an "all-expenses-paid vacation for two," I hope they have someone to go with. Those vacations probably expire after a while, and if you can't find a date, you have to take your mother.

**Read about Wormwhole on pages 31–35.

"I got free tickets. VIP tickets."

"What show?"

"We get to stay in the executive lounge."

"What show?"

"Uh . . . *The View.*"

"The View?" Pause. "I've never heard of *The View.*"

"Yeah, I know. Sorry."

I got this reaction from Ike and Owen when I called them, too. It was tough to get them excited about a show that's essentially a group of women chatting for an hour.

Owen couldn't go, so the next morning, it was just Hector, Ike, and me, meeting in the F station. I quickly assessed that we had a clothing problem. I had dressed up for *The View,* wearing a collared shirt, a belt, and Rockport shoes. Ike, who looked even buffer than the last time I'd seen him, was wearing all black, of course, with steel-toed boots. Hector had shaggy black hair, flannel-shirt-over-T-shirt, faded jeans, and sneakers. My friends weren't presentable, and somehow, the contrast between them and me made me unpresentable, too.

"Are we gonna be on TV?" Ike asked, breathless, as we piled into the F train.

"No, we're in the audience, remember?" I grabbed

a strap. "We're not guests. If everything goes right, I *might* be a guest someday."

"So, we're *not* gonna be on TV?" Hector shrugged. "Figures."

"Maybe when they do pan shots of the audience, you'll be on for, like, a tenth of a second."

"Yes!" Ike and Hector high-fived.

As we pulled into Columbus Circle, I checked someone else's watch. 10:10.

Not good. I was supposed to be at the *View* studios at 10:00, and this wasn't some appointment I could miss. This was *TV.* I punched Hector and Ike to get their attention, and we ran out of the subway toward the studio. As we passed a Barnes & Noble, I lost track of Hector. Turning around, I saw him conversing with some guy sitting on the sidewalk. "Hector!" I screamed. "Hurry!"

"Hold on, Ned! I'm talking to *Rocco!*"

"You're—you're *talking to Rocco?!*" This was too much. These people were ruining my chance for world fame. "Who the hell is *Rocco?!*"

Hector walked up to me. "Look," he whispered, "Rocco's my friend, okay? I know he looks homeless, but he's not. He just dropped out of school a few months ago—"

"Oh that's great."

"—and he doesn't really have anything to do today, y'know? So I was wondering if maybe he could have the extra ticket, y'know? The extra ticket to the show? So he can come, too? How's that sound?" Hector smiled.

I looked at Rocco. He bore a striking resemblance to Hector. He waved at me. And I figured, what the hell, we were already a motley crew. Might as well go all out.

"Okay, man," I sighed. "He can have the extra ticket."

"Really? You da man, Ned." Hector hugged me and brought Rocco over for introductions. We shook hands.

"Nice to . . . meet you, Ned." Rocco spoke slowly and openly, like he'd been shell-shocked or lobotomized, both of which seemed possible. He had rat-black hair, jeans ripped at the knee, and a decrepit backpack, which I guess he was living out of. "Where are we headed?"

"To *The View*. We're late." With Rocco in tow, we ran the next two blocks to the studio.

We entered the glass doors of ABC around 10:20. The place was packed with middle-aged women, waiting in line for their seats. Televisions were everywhere, playing the *View*-like talk show that preceded *The View*.

I approached the reception desk. "Hi, I'm Ned Vizzini. I'm here as a guest of Ronnie." I pulled out Ronnie's business card. Ike, Hector, and Rocco seemed impressed.

"Oh, Ned, we've been expecting you. Could you wait just a few minutes?"

"Sure," I turned back to my friends. "We have to wait a few minutes."

Hector was suspicious. "What happened to waiting in the *executive lounge?*"

"Yeah," Ike said. "Aren't we vee-eye-pees?"

"Uh, I guess not. Just calm down."

We stood there for fifteen minutes, talking; I got to know Rocco a little better. At some point, I noticed that Ike, who'd been very quiet, was standing in a *pool* of sweat. His entire face was dripping with it.

"Ike, are you okay?"

"Heh, heh," he smiled at me. "Forgot to take my medication this morning." He smiled again.

"You forgot your *pills?*" I never knew exactly what Ike's pills did. I just knew that the last time he hadn't taken them, we got in a fight and he locked me in his bathroom.

"Yeah," he said, wiping himself with an already sweaty hand. "It'll be fine." Hector and Rocco were talking about trends in contemporary alternative metal music.

Just then, Ronnie appeared, a young glasses-wearing guy with great hair. He strode from behind the reception desk and greeted me, the doofy white boy. I introduced him to Ike, the sweaty Mayan, and Hector and Rocco, the squatters. Ronnie grimaced but put on a game face and shook everyone's hand.

"Ike, Rocco, Hector, nice to meet you. Come this way." Ronnie motioned us to follow him to the line of audience members. Then—this was my best power trip in months—he sidestepped the line and led us down the corridor like kings. The women stared and mumbled, "Who are *they?*" There was even a velvet rope between us and the common *View* viewers.

"Wow, we're da man," Ike said.

Ronnie showed us to our front-row seats. The studio looked like heaven's living room: overstuffed couches, shiny coffee tables, and a fake New York City skyline under museum-bright lighting. The crew scurried around, putting this and that in position. But it was the audience that blew me away.

All around, filling the VIP seats next to ours, were seventy- and eighty-year-old women with pastel leisurewear (went well with the lighting) and magically immobile hair. They wore oversized earrings and parked huge purses on their laps. I listened to them chitter at each other. They had come from Maryland, North Carolina, and Florida; they couldn't wait to get back and tell their friends about the show. Some of them seemed to be in groups, like a *View* tour—all with matching shirts.

I glanced over my shoulder and saw the younger women—the ones we had passed in line before—in the back rows. It was a hierarchy: the older you were, the closer you could sit to the stage. We'd broken all the rules by being young and male; the women eyed us with total contempt.

"Okay," I told Hector, Ike, and Rocco, as a female comedian came out to warm up the crowd. "You guys behave."

"Sure, sure," they nodded. Ike was sweating. Hector and Rocco were talking about drugs. I was such an idiot for not sitting *between* my friends; from left to right, it was Rocco, Hector, Ike, me. I had no control. The show started.

The stage manager had instructed the audience to get on its feet when the theme music began, so there we were clapping as the *View* stars came out: Meredith Vieira, Star Jones, Joy Behar, and Debbie Matenopoulos, The Goddess.* My mouth dropped as she entered, a young blonde in a tight striped shirt and stretch pants.

We sat down; the hosts sat down. My friends were

---

* Very important: after this was written, Debbie Matenopoulos left *The View*; she was replaced by Lisa Ling. The move undoubtedly hurt male viewership, unless, of course, you're into Lisa Ling.

awestruck. They kept muttering about Debbie: how her shirt was too small, how they'd run up on stage and touch her if I dared them. I spent most of the next ten minutes leaning across my seat, shutting them up. Meanwhile, I tried to check out the show.

For what it was—a female romp—*The View* was decent. The women knew their parts: Meredith delivered the news, Star dismissed it, Joy joked about it, and Debbie commiserated with it. The show was well orchestrated.

After twenty minutes, my friends had settled down from the initial Debbie encounter and were behaving surprisingly well. They were quietly watching the interview with Valerie Harper—TV's "Rhoda"— and I began to think it hadn't been such a bad idea to bring them along. Then Joy announced, "Have you ever wondered what *really* turns your man on? After the commercial break, our lingerie models will demonstrate."

"*Omigod!*" Ike screamed. "Thank you, Ned!" Rocco's and Hector's faces lit up as if they'd seen the Holy Grail.

"Listen, guys!" I scolded during the commercial break, when the audience was allowed to make noise. "I am trying to get myself on this show, not get kicked out of the audience. Sit down and control yourselves and don't do anything stupid, okay? It's just—they're just gonna bring out some models, they'll do their thing, they'll leave, all right?"

Hector saluted. I laughed in spite of myself.

"Three, two, and we're on!" the bald stage manager shouted.

"Welcome back," Joy said. "Now, you may think . . ."

She kept talking, but I wasn't paying attention anymore. The models were emerging.

Except for the one who might have been a man, they were all totally stunning, with ridiculous push-up bras that made their breasts jiggle in the light. One seemed to be about fourteen; Ike, true to his vampire obsession, promised to go onstage and bite her.

The models were stone-faced as they walked the runway, but when they stopped at the end, they knew that only their torsos were being filmed, so they smiled and laughed at Joy's jokes. That was sweet; it reminded me that they were real people, not untouchable figures—that someday I might meet one and make her laugh. After they finished displaying themselves, they tightened up again, swished around, and walked back down the runway. In twenty seconds, they changed clothes behind a little curtain and repeated the process.

"Look at their backs!" Ike said. "How do they curve 'em like that?"

"Practice," Rocco answered. "Lots . . . of practice."

Near the end, the hottest model, a brunette, came out in a red satin nightie. The left side of it was off-center, revealing a little nipple.

"Dude, dude, *dude!*" Hector whimpered, loud enough to be angrily shushed by a neighboring woman.

Eventually, the models left, though it seemed to take forever to get their distracting bodies offstage. My friends were gibbering the whole time.

"How old was she?"

"Nah . . . dude . . . those were definitely real."

"Let's try to find 'em after the show. After the show, man! After the show!"

The next highlight was the musical segment. The band from *Smoky Joe's Café,* some Broadway play, performed the oldies song, "Stand By Me."

"Stand By Me" has a distinctive beat: DUN DUN, da da, DUN DUN. Well, as soon as the band hit it, the audience started clapping, accenting the DUN DUNs. Hector and Rocco clapped, too, but they messed with the beat, clapping Queen's "We Will Rock You" instead (dun dun DA, dun dun DA). I stole a look at the other side of the studio. Ronnie was glaring at me.

Now I started thinking about *The View.* I didn't see much of a future with the show; in fact, upon close inspection, I had screwed up damn near everything.

I'd arrived late, brought a bunch of delinquents, and been very disruptive throughout the broadcast. I turned to Ike and choked, "Man, there's no way I'm getting on this show."

"Oh, I thought that was clear from the beginning," he said, speaking calmly as sweat dripped off him, reminding me why he's one of my best friends. "We never even got shown on TV. Every time they filmed the audience, they cut us out."

"No kidding?" I glanced up at the cameras. "Well that's just great."

Ike resumed clapping "We Will Rock You" with Hector and Rocco. I took one last look at Ronnie and clapped along. Dun dun DA. Dun dun DA.

GOOD-BYE, OLD PAINTER

One Friday night in July, the summer between junior and senior year, James called and said he was making three hundred dollars a week doing indoor housepainting with a guy named Carlo. Did I want to help?

Now, I was looking for a computer grunt job, something I could put on my résumé and my college applications. But, as James said, Carlo was cool, he paid cash, he was in our neighborhood, and it was *painting*—how hard could *painting* be? I thought of the guys who had painted our apartment: they showed up, slopped stuff from a bucket to a wall, ate gyros for lunch, and left. So why not? I told James I'd show up for work the following Monday at 8:00 A.M.

The 8:00 A.M. thing should've been my first clue, the first tip-off that life in the paint industry was not for me. I can't be anywhere at 8:00 A.M. I'm always a little late, like 8:03, 8:07. That was okay in school, where I could chat up teachers until they forgave me. It was not okay with my new boss, Carlo.

I arrived at his work site at 8:08. I could tell it was the right place—paint chips littered the stoop.* It was a nice brownstone, like the one on *The Cosby Show*. I rang the bell and in *two seconds*—he must have been right inside, tapping his foot—Carlo appeared.

"You-a gonna come late all the time?" he said, nearly smacking me in the face as he threw open the door. "I'm-a gonna have dese *problems* with you?"

Carlo was five feet tall. I guess if you were kind, you could have pegged him at five one. But truly, he was five feet, nearly bald, with a scrunched, upturned face. His accent was deep Italian—not from Brooklyn, from Italy. If he appeared in a movie, he would be slammed as a racist stereotype. He wore a white collared shirt and white pressed pants, both covered with coats of paint drops; he held a metal implement** in his hand as if he were going to smack me with it.

"Uh, sorry."

"I know you sorry. Everybody is very, very sorry, always. But I don't have a-time for this-a *bull*crap."

Carlo led me into the brownstone—canvas on the floors, furniture covered in plastic, and a ubiquitous gasoline-type odor.

---

*When you paint a house, I learned, paint chips get *everywhere*—out on the stoop, in your clothes, in your hair. It's like they're possessed.

**It was a scraper, as I would soon learn—the tool used to remove old paint from walls, like a chisel with a flatter edge. Carlo called it "the shcrape."

"Now you and James, you-a gonna start work on the shcrape," Carlo told me. "You gonna—"

"Actually, Carlo?" James interrupted, standing by the wall wearing a baseball cap. He'd been so quiet that I hadn't noticed him.

"Hey, James," I said.

"Hey, Ned. Ah, Carlo . . . I don't think I'm going to be working with you anymore."

"What?"

"I need to go on this vacation with my family so I'll be gone next week, and now Ned's here to help you out, and . . . I just . . ."

Carlo was silent. He looked ready to explode.

"Oh, I see," he said. "You bring this guy; you decide to leave. Well, you wanna go? You go."

"Okay," James said. He nodded at me as he walked out the door.

The whole thing happened so fast; it took me a minute to realize how shafted I was. James had just left me working for an irate foreigner in a job I knew nothing about. I thought maybe I could quit, too, but Carlo was talking.

"So, you gonna start work or what? Come. Forget that guy." He gave me a paintbrush and led me upstairs.

"Now, look," he said, situating me by the brownstone's second-floor entrance. "You gotta paint this whole thing." He gestured to the foyer. "You ever painted before?"

"Yes," I lied.

Carlo looked suspicious. "Show me how you hold the brush," he ordered, crossing his stubby arms. I took the paintbrush in my fist, like the hilt of a sword.

"Oh, *goodness!* We-a gonna have problems." Carlo took the brush and scolded me like a little boy. "I ask you if you paint before, you tell me 'yes.' You can't-a even hold the brush. You paint before, huh? Yes, you paint-a your *face*. You never paint-a the *house*."

"Sorry, I—"

"Shut up! I show you. Take the brush like so."

Carlo took the brush from me so gingerly, so lightly, that it was hard to believe he'd been yelling a minute before. He held it daintily, like a pencil, with three fingers behind the handle. He traced it through the air like a fairy sprinkling magic dust.

"That is how you-a do the paint!" he said. "You gotta have-a the nice hands. Do you have-a the nice hands?"

I was totally lost. "Yes, I—"

"Take-a the brush the right way, then." I took it, trying to hold it with Carlo's ethereal grace.

"Oh my *god!* You awful! You don't know the first thing! I gonna have to train you from the beginning! You want to leave now?"

I hesitated. I did want to leave right then, but that wouldn't make me much of a man, would it. "Nah, I'll stay."

"Okay, good." Carlo's voice mellowed considerably. "You don't need to be ashamed, you just don't a-have no *eshperience*. I have forty-five years eshperience. You got none. So you have to learn, see?"

I nodded.

For the next hour, Carlo showed me how to paint. He did all the basics: dipping the brush in the bucket, tapping it against the sides three times to get the extra paint off, flipping it up to keep the paint from leaking, putting it to the wall with flat, broad strokes, or, alternately, "cutting" the wall, with the brush turned sideways to get a fine edge. He was gentle and patient, if profane.

"Now, you can't be skimpy with the paint. You gotta put a lotta paint on the wall. Like with the girls, do you do it halfway? No, you go *all* the way. Right?"

"Um, I guess."

"I gonna be back in a half hour. I want to see this room painted *good*, you hear?"

"Yeah." I dipped the brush in the paint can; as I bent down, something hit me in the head and fell to the floor. I picked it up. It was a baseball cap. Carlo had thrown it from across the room.

"*He-he-he-he-he!*" he shrieked—Carlo laughed like a four-year-old. "That's your hat. You gotta have a hat."

I put on the hat and kept painting. Within a half hour, I'd made a mess of everything. I remembered what Carlo told me, but it just wasn't working: the paint kept dripping off the brush and landing on me, running down my arms, plopping in fat drops on my hat.* Carlo returned as I was doing the ceiling, trying desperately not to fall off the ladder.

"Mama *mia!*" (He really said that; I wouldn't make it up.) "I could take my money, throw it *away,* and still, it's cheaper than you, because I don't have to clean up after you! I give you an *hour,* and you not done with the room. You work like an *old man!*"

That ended up being one of Carlo's favorite lines. "You like an old man; *I* supposed to be the old man. You not just a hundred-year-old man. You a hun-dred-*twenty*-year-old man!"

"Come, we'll find something else for you to do." Carlo led me up the brownstone's staircase. "You see these?"

I couldn't see too well because the baseball cap

---

*Despite that hat—I'll never know how—lots of paint ended up in my *hair,* and it wouldn't wash out in the shower. I had to wait for weeks until it wore out.

covered my eyes. Carlo was pointing to the spindles that held up the banister. The house was four stories high so there were at least one hundred of these decorative posts.

"You gotta paint all these," Carlo said. "*White.* If you-a get paint on the steps, I kill you. If you-a let paint drip downstairs, on the rugs, I kill you. You spill, I kill you. Okay?"

"Yup." I had done a more precise estimate. There were one hundred fifty spindles. The job would take days.

"Get started." Carlo left to do Carlo things. I began with the first spindle.

• • •

Three hours later—and it wasn't a bad three hours, once I got into the pace of things—Carlo came back upstairs.

"Hey, you do a-pretty good!" he nodded, inspecting my work. "No drips, good. Time for lunch." I leapt down the stairs, careened out of the brownstone, and ran down the block, still pretty much covered in paint. I bought an iced coffee, some lemon pound cake, and a newspaper from Connecticut Muffin (a local trendy coffee shop), then sprinted back to the brownstone to eat. Carlo was there on the stoop with a sandwich.

"What you got?" he asked, pointing at my newspaper.

"Oh, this, it's just something for me to read at lunch."

"You read, huh?"

"Yeah."

"I don't care for the reading," he said, fluttering his hands. I dug into my pound cake. "The reading, it's not for me. It's-a bull*crap*."

"*Hmmm*, yeah," I mumbled, while chewing. So Carlo didn't read. He was making thousands of dollars a week. Nothing for me to judge.

"The people who read, they a-think they know everything, but they don't-a got no common *shense*. Like you. I know you a smart guy;* I know from the beginning, but you ain't-a got no common *shense* at all."

"Uh, thanks." I was engrossed in my newspaper and was already learning to tune out Carlo when he got insulting.

"You gonna go to college?" he asked. "What college?"

I had an automatic response to that. Whenever anyone asked me about college, I got it out of the way—quickly. "Probably Harvard."

---

*Getting compliments from Carlo was much tougher than getting blood from a stone. It was like getting, I don't know, a full-featured fax machine from a stone. I was very proud when he complimented me.

"Not a good idea. You gotta go to the college a *common shense! He-he-he-he-he!* C'mon, no more lunch. More work."

I went back inside and did fifteen more spindles. Carlo didn't let me leave until 6:00, which meant I had worked a ten-hour day with a half-hour lunch break. I trudged home (the three-block walk was a lot longer than it had been that morning) and vegged out in front of the TV for four hours. Then I slept.

The next day, I learned the horrible secret of painting: you can't change clothes. Everything you wear on the job is going to get ruined, so unless you have five outfits to burn, you wear one pair of pants and one shirt the whole week. The sweat of each day dries in your clothes, and the next day, the clothes *themselves* begin to sweat, old sweat blending with new, everything blending with the sweet gasoline smell of the paint.

The second day, I worked with rollers. Now, it's easy to use a roller in some art class;* it's a lot harder to put one on a six-foot stick and cover a ceiling with an even coat of primer.** I moved too fast: paint flew off my roller in evil drops, landing in my hair and on

---

*Art class was something I lost all respect for in my painting career. When you slop noxious oil-based gunk from bucket to wall for eight hours plus, the thought of painting for fun becomes stomach churning. I challenge any art student reading this to paint your own house—you'll end up a mutual-fund analyst.

**Basic terminology: primer is the white paint that you put on a surface before you put the final, colored paint on. Primer has to be totally even.

wood cabinets, which I had to clean very quickly to avoid decapitation by Carlo.

My boss started asking me about my love life on day two. "You have a girlfriend?" Carlo said while I painted with the roller.

"Yes," I lied. If I said no, I'd probably get yelled at.

"Well, that's nice," he mused. "I hope she is a beautiful flower. Like my wife, a beautiful flower."

Carlo had two classifications for the women of the world: "fake women" and "beautiful flowers." When we sat on the brownstone's stoop for lunch (never ate anywhere else), he would gesture at women passing by.

"You see that? She is disgusting! The lips, the nose—all fake. Not real. Not nice to touch, not at all. I can tell." I would nod.

Or, "There! Now that is a beautiful flower. Look at-a how she moves. Natural like the wind." Carlo could get quite romantic. "Like my wife. You want just to hold her. A beautiful flower."

I could never tell the difference between the beautiful flowers and the fake women. It bothered me. I would have someone pegged as a fake woman, and then Carlo would christen her a beautiful flower; I'd have to take a second look. He was always right.

Another painter, Carmello, came in on alternate

days. Carmello was like a young Carlo with hair. He loved the "Lite FM" radio station. He would only paint a room if Lite FM was on, and he sang along with it in a spectacularly out-of-tune voice. He called me "Joe": "Hey, Joe, bring me the wide scraper." "You did a nice job on these banister things, Joe." "Don't forget to clean out the sink, Joe." I got used to it.

Working for Carlo, however, was mostly not cutesy anecdotes. It was abuse. If he thought I was working too slow, he would come up behind me and hit me—never very hard—and curse at me. I withstood it; I figured it was just part of growing up, having a malevolent, profane dwarf boss who disdained reading. Mostly, I thought of payday, Friday, when I would receive those crisp one-hundred-dollar bills.

But Friday afternoon was a long time coming, especially in the same clothes I'd been wearing all week, and by 5:00, when Carlo opened his astonishingly thick wallet to hand me three hundred dollars, it just wasn't worth it anymore.

In a movie, I would have stayed with Carlo. I would have taught him how to read; he would have taught me how to seduce beautiful flowers. I would have mellowed him out; he would have toughened me up. We would have learned from each other—the hardened foreigner and the self-important kid—and, in the end, I would be crying at his funeral. Instead, I called Hector.

"Dude," I said. "It's Ned, and I have this great job, if you want it. I can't really do it anymore. . . ."

GETTING SLOPPY
WITH POPPY

I met Poppy over the summer. I was going to a birthday party in the Village. On my way, walking down East Fourth Street, I passed four Hispanic guys playing dominoes. They were on the sidewalk, sitting in folding chairs at a makeshift table, keeping score on an old Marlboro carton. Their leader was this wild-haired, shirtless old man with thick round glasses.

I'd learned how to play dominoes a year before, while interning at my parents' office. So I stopped, leaned against a car, and watched. I wasn't there ten seconds before Poppy smiled at me.

"Hey, you wanna play?"

I suspected treachery. Maybe they were hustlers. "Um . . . I don't have any money."

"*So?* We don't play for money—we play for fun. Sit down!"

Poppy got up. I took his seat. "You want something to drink, my friend?" he asked, patting my shoulder. "Beer? Soda?"

"No, thanks." I didn't feel comfortable taking beer

from this guy just yet. Besides, I wouldn't have time for beer. I was only going to play one game.

He grabbed my hand. "The people, they call me Poppy. Wha's your name?"

I couldn't tell him it was Ned. Too dorky. If I was going to play dominoes with these guys, I needed a new name, something edgy and streetwise.

"Skitch," I said. I'd always wanted to be called Skitch.

"Skitch?" he snorted. "No, *cabron*,* what is your *real* name?"

Okay, so Skitch was too fake. I needed something neutral.

"John."

"John, my new friend, welcome!" Poppy raised his head to the sky. I sensed a ritual coming on. "Yes, welcome to East Fourth Street, *the capital of the world!* You wanna beer?"

This time I said yes.

Two hours later, I was still there.** For those of you who've never played dominoes, the game is like hearts or bridge. You play in teams of two; the strategy is figuring out what the other players are holding.

---

* *Cabron* means "goat" in Spanish. It's an all-purpose insult.

** I never did get to the birthday party I was going to. The girl hosting it was angry with me.

It's addictive, especially when accompanied by free beer, which Poppy never stopped providing. As my new friend handed me a second, third, and fourth Bud—no questions asked—I began to understand how things worked on East Fourth Street. Poppy was the king. He had free rein at the *bodegas:** he could have complimentary chips, salsa, beer, gum, whatever. If I offered to pay for these items, he would give an automatic staccato response: "No, *cabron*, everything has been bought and paid for in *full!*"

The other players were almost as entertaining as Poppy. We had Fumo, the silent Confucius look-alike who sat in for two games and left promptly, as if he had a meeting to get to. Poppy said he was homeless. Then there was Old Tony or Old Frankie—I forget which—a timeless geezer who kept a cigarette drooping from his lips at all times and didn't seem to care if it was lit.

Other members of the East Fourth Street community came to see Poppy—not to play dominoes, but to pay tribute. They slapped him on the back, made sure he was doing all right, gave him beer, talked about the weather, and left with a handshake.

---

*Bodegas are little shops scattered all over New York. The Mini Mart where I'd bought beer with Owen (pages 106–115) was a bodega.

Sometimes, to Poppy's delight, they asked him about President Clinton and Monica.*

Poppy had strong opinions about the Clinton and Monica scandal. Whenever someone mentioned it, he began howling, "*Clinton y Mooonica! Ayyy!* I tell you, these Republicans, *cabron*, awful. They try to kill the president for nothing! Clinton, he did not even do it to her, just a little thing with a cigar!" The cigar was of particular interest. Poppy would rhapsodize about it. "He should have smoked it! Destroy the evidence! *Aaaa!*"

I stayed at East Fourth Street for three hours that day, and I made a point of coming back all through August and September. I liked Poppy; I loved dominoes; I didn't mind the free beer;** I enjoyed spending my time with nutty old men; and for the low, low round-trip price of three dollars subway fare, this wasn't a bad way to spend a summer evening.

One Saturday, a homeless black dude with a shopping cart came by the dominoes table.

"Major!" Poppy greeted him, jumping up. "Major, long time we have not seen you. Meet my new best friend, ah, wha's your name?"

---

*Ho boy, if you don't know about Clinton and Monica (or "Clinton y Monica," as Poppy would say), look them up. One of our truly great political scandals.

**You'd think I'd get in trouble as a minor openly drinking beer in the street, but the cops never came to East Fourth

Poppy needed to be retold my fake name every time I visited. "John," I said.

"Ah, yes, John. John, meet Major."

I shook his hand.

"Ya wanna see my cart, right?" Major asked. I nodded.

Major led me into the street and beckoned me to a shopping cart. Like many homeless people, he made his living filling his cart with bottles and recycling them. "Ain't you never heard of Major's cart?" he beamed. "I got the best cart in the city. Man, this here's the *Cadillac* of carts."

I had to admit it was nifty. He had partitioned it with wooden planks, sorting his bottles by color. "Nobody messes with my cart, man. They just see it, and they go, 'Hey, that's Major's cart!' and they leave it alone. You know how much weight I can pull in this cart?"

"Forty pounds."

"Twenty-one *hundred* pounds, man! I pulled that much when the cops was chasing me."

"That's a lot of bottles."

"Damn right. Thing was full."

Another time, a friend of Poppy's came by the table and introduced himself as the world-famous French ballet composer, "Pierre." (He gave me his business card. It read, "Pierre. Dance.") I also shook hands with a self-proclaimed descendant of Peter Stuyvesant, who said he'd made millions in currency trading. ("Yeah, a millionaire, right, so what is he doing here?" Poppy asked.)

But in late September, I stopped going to play dominoes. It got cold, so no one showed up anymore. Also, I had to go to school.

Around December 23, I returned to East Fourth Street looking for Poppy. I wanted to wish him a Merry Christmas, plus I craved a real game with Fumo and Old Frankie (or Old Tony). Poppy wasn't out on the sidewalk—it was far too cold—but I found him in the back room of his favorite bodega, sitting at a folding table. A jagged scar ran down his forehead, the stitches still in place.

"Whoa, Poppy, what happened to you?"

"Ay, *cabron*," he smiled at me. "You come at a bad time." He pointed at his face. "I get stabbed in the head with a bottle."

"What?"

"Yes, yes, with a *bottle!* Happened a few days ago. These drug dealers come to my block; they mess with me."

"Oh, man." I sat down next to him.

"It's not bad," Poppy said, waving his hands at

me. "It's shown me many things. For example, my friend, I have stopped with the bottle. It is no good for my health. No good for my pocketbook."

I couldn't believe it; Poppy could pack away a lot of beers.

"No more!" he yelled, standing up. Then he sat down and pulled me close. "You know, John"—this was the first time he remembered my name, I swear—"They used to call me a 'street father.' I am friendly to everyone, get people things, right? Not anymore. Too much drug dealers, too much every- thing, I get *stabbed in the head*." He pointed to his wound. "Now I say, let these people buy their own beer! Let everybody play dominoes by themselves! Merry Christmas!"

Poppy stood up, drew himself a glass of water, and turned on his radio to the Spanish station.

"I like you very much, John," he told me. "But it's no more dominoes for a while."

"Okay." Not much I could say. I shook his hand. "Feel better, I guess."

As I walked out of the bodega, Poppy told me I could have some free chips, so I took barbecue. I had this urge to tell him my real name. I turned around to do so, more than once, but I was too embarrassed— of my real name and of the fact that I'd lied for so long.

METROCARDED

I was ashamed of the NYPD. Turnstile jumping is the sort of crime they've vowed to rub out, but there I was, having jumped to and from Manhattan for an entire summer, and nothing. No cops. No alarms. No token booth ladies kicking open their doors and chasing me down. Truth is, I was reassured when I got caught.

It was a Friday night; I was leaving a disappointing local concert with my semiconscious friend Hector. It was warm and misty out; for some reason, a lot of people were fighting. On our way to the subway, we saw a scruffy white guy hit a businessman with an umbrella and two huge black dudes with cell phones throwing punches outside a bar.

"You know, Hec," I said as we approached the F train, "I have no money."

He shrugged. "I have enough for one token."

I wasn't listening: I was confessing. "Hec, I really don't want to jump tonight. I've jumped too much lately. It's the law of averages. I'm gonna get caught sooner or later."

He repeated, "I have enough for one token. You

can slip in after me." But I don't like slipping in after people. It looks stupid, plus you can give your hip a nasty bang on the turnstile.

We headed into the F station; I picked up speed. You don't need a running start to jump turnstiles, but it goes more smoothly that way. I flew by the token booth, planted my hands over the MetroCard slits, and vaulted sweetly over the bars. Hector did the same, even though he had money.

As soon as my feet hit the ground, I heard the cops yelling, "*Hey!* Yeah, *you two!*"

I stopped. I'd seen this coming, hadn't I? I flashed forward through the consequences: me explaining my arrest to my parents, me with a criminal record, unable to get a good job, kicked out of high school, living on the street. But if I was apologetic and nice, maybe I'd come out okay.

I looked at the cops. Damn, they looked like cops. Both were Italian; one, a pudgy guy in his forties; the other, young and jumpy. They had brown hair and mustaches. They were in plainclothes. At some point, they must have produced badges, but they didn't need to. They were movie cops, perfect for the part.

"C'mere," the young, jumpy one said. He was standing in front of an open chrome door, one of those unlabeled doors in subway stations, which I had thought led to janitor's closets. There were little slits in the door, and I realized: the cops had been *sitting* in there! They stared through those slits all day, keeping watch for offensive citizens. It was a setup!

Hector and I walked through the door. There was a room with a table, a bench, a lot of pipes, and some cop stuff like radios and jackets. The young officer aimed himself at Hector, the older one turned to me. They both pulled out pads of paper.

"How old are you?" mine asked.

"Seventeen," I nodded as I said it.

"And how old are you?" Hector's cop asked, shaking his pen.

"Uh . . ." Hector seemed really flustered. "Sixteen—no wait, I mean seventeen."

"*Excuse me?* Is it sixteen or seventeen?"

"Seventeen."

"Are you *sure?*"

"Yeah. I get a little confused because I just turned—"

"I hope you're not lying to me. Because I don't like being *lied* to. If you start that, we're gonna have problems."

"I know you don't believe me—"

"You're right. I *don't* believe you." Now it was

181

clear. Just like in the movies: there was a nice cop and a mean one, and Hector had gotten the mean one.

"What school do you go to?" my cop asked. His nameplate said, "Patillo."

"Stuyvesant." I showed my I.D. card.* Patillo studied it.

"What does that say?" He pointed at the lettering. The words were in an unintelligible gothic font—to give my school some class, I guess.

"It says 'Stuyvesant High School.'" I indicated each word.

"How come they write it that way?" he sounded suspicious, as if I'd faked the card.

"I dunno."

"Any other I.D.?"

I emptied my pockets. Standard nerd fare: a paperback version of *The Two Towers*, a floppy disk, a graphing calculator. Patillo eyed the calculator as if it were a bomb. He wrote down my address and my phone number and told me to sit down next to Hector, who'd finished his interview.

"You guys sit tight. We're putting a call in to headquarters to find out what to do with you," the jumpy cop said. He and Patillo walked out, leaving me alone with Hector. We twiddled our thumbs—literally, like

---

*This was the same I.D. that duped the Mini Mart clerk back when I was a sophomore (pages 106–115).

in a Norman Rockwell painting: *Caught Jumping Turnstiles*. Hector traced patterns in the bench with his fingernail.

"What are they gonna do to us?" I asked him.

"I think we get a ticket. Like a parking ticket."

"Do we get a criminal record?"

"Nah. Not unless they fingerprint us."

I started calculating the economics. A token costs a dollar fifty; I'd jumped turnstiles since June, which meant maybe forty free rides. So as long as my ticket was less than sixty bucks, I would come out ahead. That was comforting.

"All right, kids," the two officers said as they returned. "You're both old enough to be issued summonses so you're getting summonses. We'll notify your parents of this incident by mail." Well, that wasn't going to be fun, but I'd live. I was handed a sixty-dollar ticket that looked exactly like a parking violation.

"As for *you*," the mean cop said, turning to Hector. "Don't you *ever* lie about your age to a police officer. You do not know how close I was to taking you down to central booking. Do you have *any idea* what that's like? Do you have *any idea* how humiliating it is to be brought in and strip-searched? To spread your cheeks?" I had known that was coming. Before we could be released, the cops had to bring up the most compelling threat of our justice system: spreading one's cheeks.

"You're free to go." They opened the chrome door and shooed us out. I glanced at my ticket and started to chuckle. *Exactly* sixty dollars. Which meant I was repaying my debt to society, give or take a buck. I felt clean, like I should pay the ticket right there. I was proud of the police, and New York in general, for catching me.

"What are you laughing at?" Hector asked.

I couldn't tell him the sappy stuff so I said, "You know, Hec, high school and summer camp and girls are all different from the way they are on TV. But cops. Cops are exactly the same."

SENIOR YEAR

FORCED MARCH

I should have spent the summer before senior year volunteering in a soup kitchen or practicing violin five hours a day, but instead I disrupted a television show, played a lot of dominoes, and painted houses with a guy named Carlo. That didn't serve me well when it came time to apply for college.

The colleges, you see, want a lot these days. They don't just want you to be a good student. They don't just want dedication, good-naturedness, and self-sacrifice. They want you to be *angular*. That's a real term; I read about it in *The Wall Street Journal*. Today's colleges are looking for angular students—passionate about a field of interest they've discovered in high school. They don't want well-rounded; they want you to be exclusively devoted to one thing—if you say you're into computers, you'd better have won some high-tech award.

I could have been angular, no question about it. I could have written for the school newspaper, been an active member of whatever literary clubs Stuyvesant had, or attended readings in the library.

But I never had time. I was doing far more important things:

FRESHMAN YEAR
- Played a lot of Magic: The Gathering.
- Got really, really good at sliding down escalator
  handrails.
- Wrote a science fiction story that appeared in the
  very back of Stuy's science fiction magazine.
- Entered the Scholastic Writing Awards, winning
  an award for, uh, honorable mention.*

SOPHOMORE YEAR
- Spent a year and a half on the math team, then
  left because it got too hard.**
- Joined the computer science team, where I
  learned a lot about computers and a lot more
  about *The Simpsons.*

JUNIOR YEAR
- Continued not to participate in team sports of any
  kind.
- Began writing and self-publishing a profane
  comic book called *Uncle Tumba.*

---

*Details of the award are given in "Horrible Mention" (pages 59–64).

** Sample problem from math team: "Find the smallest prime that is the fifth term of an increasing arithmetic sequence, all four of the preceding terms also being prime."

- Failed at a run for class president on a ticket with someone who had the same initials as me. (That was the big selling point—we were both "NV," and our signs read "eNVy us!")

At the beginning of my junior year, I was dragged along with eight hundred other juniors to the Stuyvesant theater, to hear our college advisor tell us how to get into college. I remember very little about the event because I was reading *Rising Sun.** But I do remember scrunching in my seat, jotting notes on the book's inside cover, and thinking, "Here you are, Ned. This is the last race. If you were in a sitcom, you'd be going all sappy and moralistic before the final laughs. You are finally, truly, going to get out of high school, and if you work hard enough and get into a Good College, you'll end up with a sweatshirt, a bumper sticker, and a fulfilling life."

That evening, I approached Mom and Dad in the living room.

"Okay, guys," I told them. "We need to talk about college."

"Thank God," Dad said. He was playing Tetris, and he didn't look up. "When are you leaving?"

"Jim!" Mom scolded. "What do we need to know, honey?"

---

*A book by Michael Crichton, author of *Jurassic Park,* RIP.

I pulled out my comprehensive notes from the college meeting and read them off:

(1) Take SATs.
(2) Take Achievements.
(3) Get teacher recommendations.
(4) Get an SSR.
(5) Fill out applications.

"That's all I have to do," I added.

"Is this about money?" Dad asked. "How much money do you want?"

"Ignore him," Mom told me. "Ned, as far as I can see, you have no problems. You'll take the SATs and do fine; you'll take the Achievements and do fine. And you can get teacher recommendations. What's an SSR?"

"Secondary School Recommendation. That's, like, a big departmental recommendation that they do for you."

"Right! So you have everything covered! Do you want a tutor for the SATs?"

"Yeah." I didn't want one, but I figured a tutor might motivate me for this whole muddy deal.

Dad actually paused Tetris and looked up. "Why are you going through this charade of applying to different schools?" he asked. "Don't you only want to go to Harvard?"

"Uh . . ." I didn't like it that Dad knew me so well.

"Oh yes, I know. I was once like you. You have to go to the *best* school, don't you?"

"Jim!" Mom exclaimed. "Leave him alone! Harvard is *not* 'the best school,' for goodness' sake."

"You want that grand intellectual—what do they call it?—bitch slap, don't you, Ned? You want to prove that you're smarter than not just 90, not just 99, but *99.9* percent of your generation."

"I guess." He had me there.

"Well, then." Dad returned to Tetris. "Apply to Harvard. You apply, you get in, and it's all settled. You don't need a tutor. I took the GREs cold and got eight hundred on the math part. And that was before all this grade-curving."

That winter the mail started coming. University of Oklahoma, Pitzer, Albany . . . brochures, postcards, "inside looks," newspaper clippings, excerpts from *U.S. News & World Report* . . . papers from schools clogged our apartment every day. That's not to mention the secondary mail: letters from test-prep centers, scholarship search services, tutors, seminars, and "college agents" who would handle the whole process for me as if it were taxes.

That spring, I had my first meeting with my personal college advisor, Dr. Arnold. Stuyvesant gave every student an advisor to ease us through the college process. Dr. Arnold was tall, bearded, kind-hearted, and quiet.

"Well, Ned," he said as I sat in his office after class. He put his index fingers together and wiggled them under his nose, like the Grinch. "Where would you like to go to school?"

There was a prevailing notion in American high schools at the time that students must apply to seven colleges: two "dream schools" (the ones you want to go to), three "middle-of-the-road schools" (the ones you wouldn't mind going to), and two "safety schools" (at least you're going to college). The idea of applying to just a couple of schools you're interested in was long dead. It's easy to understand why. With the seven-school system, the colleges received thousands of dollars more in application fees. And the high schools could maneuver even the least promising kids into safety schools, boasting a higher percentage of students who "move to pursue their education."

I gave him my list, with Harvard at the top.

"Okay," Dr. Arnold nodded, taking notes. "What have you done that you would like me to mention in your SSR?"

I began to list my accomplishments and found them lacking. Dr. Arnold wasn't fazed. "I'll emphasize the things that will help you and ignore the things that won't," he said, dismissing me from his office. "Just worry about the SATs—and see if you can do something over the summer."

Right, the SATs.* On May 15, I took them, which brings me to the final demon of the application process: the College Board. See, the SATs, Achievements, and whatnot are created and administered by a private organization that makes gobs of money off the misery of high school students. The College Board schedules the tests, tells you where to take them, and proceeds to charge fees. First, you pay a fee for taking the exams. Then you pay a fee if you register "late" for the exams (late being an abstract period determined by the College Board). Once you've taken your tests, you pay a fee for sending your scores to the appropriate colleges, and, of course, if you send these "late," you pay an additional "rush" fee. Want to change your test date? Fee. Cancel your scores? Fee. I'd say the College Board sucked three hundred dollars out of my family. I'm waiting for the IPO.

In June, I resolved to clear up all my college stuff: fill out the forms, register for the tests, apply for scholarships. None of that happened, though. I was too busy playing dominoes in the street and inhaling noxious fumes as an apprentice housepainter. The

*I got a 1530, a score I lied about almost as much as my virginity. I found that if I told people I got higher than a 1400, they'd get angry.

only thing I did do was buy the Princeton Review's *Best 311 Colleges*, which informed me that Harvard was really, really hard to get into. By then, it was time to go back to school.

Now, as I was beginning senior year, I had one important decision to make. Should I apply early? Early admission allows a student to commit to a "dream school" and avoid the hassle of applying elsewhere. Here's how it works: in November of your senior year, you apply to your favorite college. The admissions office reviews your application quickly, handing down its decision within a month. The school does one of three things: accepts you, in which case you're legally obligated to attend; rejects you; or defers you, putting off the question of your admission until the following April.

I wanted to apply early to Harvard. I didn't even want to go there anymore—when I visited the school I saw too many eyebrow rings and not enough human activity. But, oh man, I wanted to get in. I wanted that grand intellectual bitch slap, like Dad said. Besides, Harvard had a special clause: I could refuse the school even after getting in early. That's what I *really* wanted.

I filled out the Harvard forms the night before they were due. There were two parts, inspiringly titled Part I and Part II. Part I was basic information:

age, gender, intended major—it was easy to complete. Part II, however, requested an essay and more detailed personal information—it was a killer. Part II had a whole page for extracurricular activities, which I was hard-pressed to fill, and at the bottom of the page it suggested: "If you have participated in other activities that you would like us to know about, feel free to attach another sheet." Right.

By 6:00 A.M. I'd written in two different-colored pens and smudged Whiteout everywhere, but I'd finished the form. I showed it to Mom. She had a fit.

"You *cannot* send this to *Harvard!*" We were in the kitchen, huddled over the application as if it were an eviction notice. "Ned, it looks like it was written on a moving train!"

"I know, sorry."

"And you didn't even mention church! How could you not say that you were *president* of your *church youth group?*"

"Mom, that was in *eighth grade!*"

"Oh, they don't care. Gimme that Whiteout." Within an hour, Mom had completely redone the application. There were now *two* kinds of handwriting on it, in *three* different colors of ink, and, apparently, I was a volunteer in the Parks Department and a student coordinator for Meals on Wheels.*

---

* "That's not lying," Mom said. "Just emphasizing."

"There," she summed up, *"that's* how you fill out an application."

I mailed it on my way to school.

Two weeks later, I got a letter.

HARVARD UNIVERSITY

Ned Vizzini,

We at Harvard have received your application for admission, but we have not yet received your application fee of forty dollars. Please send it promptly.

I showed the letter to Mom, and she delivered her usual words of encouragement, "My goodness, Ned, we've really done it this time, huh? We sent in an application that looked like the handiwork of a six-year-old, *and* we forgot to include the check. Harvard won't even *look* at you."

But they did. Two weeks later, I had the interview.

It was an utter disaster. I showed up an hour late because I thought it was on Thirty-fourth Street instead of Forty-fourth.* My interviewers, two young women named Suzie and Ann, sat me down in a plush room, introduced themselves as Harvard grads, and grilled me gently for an hour. Mostly, we talked about stocks, but near the end of the interview, I made the grave error of pulling out the *Uncle Tumba* comic.

Uncle Tumba, my foray into self-publishing, was a comic book about an elderly vagrant from ancient Tibet who roamed the countryside seeking adventure. I had started it with a friend, Adam, and we'd sold nearly two hundred copies at our school.

"Cool, I love comics!" Suzie said, when I told her about it. "May I see?"**

I handed over issue number one. She began to read it. Her face immediately clouded.

"There are curses in here."

"Well, yeah," I explained. "I could always tone down the cursing, though. In future issues."

"Can we keep copies?" Ann asked.

"Sure," I said. "One dollar each."

Suzie and Ann gaped at me. "You're going to charge us?"

"Well, uh, I wouldn't want it to seem like I was trying to bribe my way into Harvard!" It was a lame

---

* The Harvard lady really said "Thirty-fourth" on the phone. I think she knew, even then, that I wasn't going to get in and was just messing with me.

** She really said that—"May I." My interviewers were perfect.

joke, but there was no way I was giving away those issues for free. I needed the money for orange Hostess cupcakes on the way home.

From that moment on, the college process moved pretty quickly. In December, Harvard deferred me. I applied to my other schools—with a bit more care—in January. The final tally came in April: rejected by Harvard and Yale, accepted everywhere else.

There must have been a moment where I kissed the big schools good-bye—a split second spent watching late-night television, instead of studying, that pushed me into rejection territory. Who knows when it was? I'd like to think I spent it doing something fun.

FUN IN THE SUN

The setup was perfect. Too perfect. On April 4, I was going to turn eighteen. On that same date, I was scheduled to be in Cancún, Mexico, on my high school senior trip. That deserved its own rock song; I'd be sitting on the beach at noon, waking up to face the tropical sun, with a gorgeous brunette on a towel by my side. She'd hand me a Corona with a wedge of lime and say, "Happy birthday, Ned. You're *eighteen*." And then she'd smile.

Didn't exactly work out that way.

I heard about the Cancún trip in the fall of senior year. I didn't have any idea what it was. I was ignorant of the whole senior trip ritual, where wealthy teenagers with lenient parents escape to warm climates to get drunk and have casual sexual encounters. I'd just hear it whispered, "Cancún." "Man, this homework sucks. I can't wait to go to Cancún." "I hate school. The only reason I'm still here is for Cancún."

One day, Owen, my bug-eyed Russian friend, approached me in the hall and asked outright, "Dude, are you going to Cancún?"

"Probably," I said. That was good. "Probably"

made me sound cool—like I'd known about the trip all along—but it was noncommittal. I didn't want to commit to this before I knew what it was.

"All *right*," Owen said, throwing his arm around me.

I broke his mood by asking the nerdiest possible question. "Uh, what is Cancún? Exactly?"

"Stupid, it's the senior trip. We fly down to Mexico to party for a week."

"Oh. How many people?"

"Whoever can afford it, like forty, fifty people. Lots of girls is the important thing."

"How much does it cost?"

"Eight hundred bucks."

"Damn."

"Dude, are you going or not? And don't tell me you can't afford it. You're probably the only guy in the school who *can* afford it, since you've got your own money. What do you have by now? A hundred thousand dollars?" Owen was exaggerating. I had about ten thousand dollars saved up at this time; no way was I spending 8 percent on some trip.

"I'm just saying, eight hundred bucks is a lot of money."

"Ned, you *want* to do this. I know you do. I'm telling you now so you can room with me and Josh and Alex."

I sighed.

"Dude, we *need* somebody else to room with us."

I knew this could be trouble.

"I'll go."

"Okay!" Owen grinned. "So go talk to Emily! She's, like, the coordinator. She has sheets for you to fill out."

"Cool."

Talking to Emily wasn't going to be fun. She was one of those criminally gorgeous high school girls; she made me feel about eight years old. If she found out I was going on her trip, she'd laugh in my face. I sought her out a couple of days later.

"Hey, Emily?" She was sitting with the other preppy seniors in their segregated area by the Snapple machine. "I'm, uh, going to Cancún, and I need some literature?"

"Oh, Ned, you're going?" Her smile was too wide. And she had said my name, which was suspect—I didn't even think she *knew* my name. "Here, let me give you the sheet."

She handed me a colorful piece of paper. "This," she bubbled, "has all the info! About the trip! See! The name of the company is Student Travel Services; the trip costs eight hundred fifty dollars; we leave on April second . . ."

I wasn't looking where Emily was pointing, though. I was checking out the flyer's photo: a row of thonged butts under the caption, "Fun in the Sun."

"Okay?" Emily summed up whatever she'd been telling me.

"Yeah." I folded the flyer neatly, tucked it in my pocket, and took it home to show my mother. "Mom," I said, closing the door and throwing my backpack on the dining room table. She was sitting with her feet up, doing a crossword puzzle.

"Hi, honey," she said, looking at me. "How was your day?"

"Good, good . . . ah, Mom, I have to show you this." I pushed the "Fun in the Sun" flyer in front of her. "I'm going to Cancún in April."

"*Whaaat?*" Mom jumped from her chair, clutching her crossword like a shield. The flyer dropped to the ground. *"Whaaaaat?!"*

"It's spring break! I've done very well in school. I deserve a reward, right? It's just, you know, a vacation. To Cancún."

"Vacation? Ha! It's an *orgy of sex and drugs!*" She grabbed the flyer off the floor and inspected it.

"It's *not* an orgy of sex and drugs." I was wistful. "It won't be for me, anyway."

But now Mom had seen the thongs. *"Look* at

this!" she howled. "No, no, no, no, no, no, *no!*" Uh-oh, the Seven Nos. Those were always a bad sign. "You are absolutely—"

For the next few minutes, we had an interesting scene. Mom yelled at me about Cancún and I yelled back, but the problem was, she was right. The place *was* a seedy hole, and when I tried to describe it as anything else ("There are ruins, Mom, I'll see the Cancún ruins!"), she would burst out laughing. Then I would chuckle, despite myself, until our shouting degenerated into laughter. At some point, I noticed that our apartment door was open; it always opened while we fought, delivering the action in stereo to our neighbors.

I closed the door and gave in. "Okay, fine, Mom," I smiled. "You won't let me have a wholesome time in Cancún. I guess I'll have to suffer."

She sat back down. "Don't try to pull one over on me, Ned," she said. "I was young once, too."

I walked to my room, plopped down on my bed, and started strategizing. How could I get to Cancún without Mom finding out?

It wasn't such a stretch. I'd snuck out on my parents before and lied about my whereabouts to stay at parties. The method was always the same:

Me: "Mom, I'm sleeping over at James's house tonight."

Mom: "You are? Oh, how is James? Is he doing okay?"

Me: "He's fine, Mom. I'm sure he says hi."

Mom: "Well, if you're going there, leave the phone number by the stove so I don't have to look it up if I want to call."

Then I'd leave the phone number—James's legitimate phone number—and head out, knowing she'd never call. We had a tacit pact—if I showed enough respect to give her a phone number, she'd show enough respect not to check on me.

Cancún would operate on the same principle, but for a week, instead of a night. I'd tell Mom and Dad that I was staying at James's *country* house this time. The plan was airtight; I actually had stayed there a year before so the element of parental trust was in place. I'd give my parents a phone number, and they wouldn't call. I'd be home free—eighteen, on the blanket with my beach babe, as planned.

I went to school the next day with an eight-hundred-fifty-dollar Cancún deposit. I handed it to Emily by the Snapple machine.

"You know, it's *so great* that you're going, Ned," she said earnestly.

Emily's act was beginning to bother me. If she liked me—which would be unthinkably cool—I needed to move fast. I'd found that girls, when they developed crushes, were never receptive for more than two weeks. Sure, they'd *remember* a crush for two years and then tell you, "Ned, back in sophomore year, I thought you were *sooo* cute." But they were only open for two weeks—you needed to act quick.

"You're really glad I'm going?" I asked Emily. "I mean, *glad* glad?"

"Oh, *yeah*," she said. "You round out a whole room. It's you, Owen, Alex, and Josh. And I get paid by the room."

"You do?"

"Uh-huh. It's a sponsorship. The company sending everyone to Cancún pays me based on how many people go. I am making *so much money*. You wouldn't believe it."

"Oh." Glad I got that cleared up.

• • •

I went through the dark months—November, December, January—without any changes on the Cancún front. My escape plan stayed the same: (1) leisurely tell my parents I was going to spend the week at James's country house; (2) get on the plane; (3) party; (4) pray for no phone calls. But at the end of January, two things happened: I took on the role of Jesus, and I got a girlfriend.

Jesus first, though I assure you, I was more

surprised to get the girlfriend. My church, St. John's, which Mom had made me attend all through adolescence, held an annual Easter Passion, a re-enactment of Christ's crucifixion, with congregation members playing the major characters. St. John's liked to cast teenagers* in the Jesus role—I don't know why; we were singularly unqualified to play the pure-minded son of God, but whatever. For two years, my friend John had played Jesus, but that year, he declined. Because there was no one else to play the part and (much more significantly) because Mom pressured me, I took it.

As for the girlfriend, wow. Her name was Judith, and she was everything I'd missed in high school—love, status, constant physical attention—wrapped up and delivered in a slick, beautiful package. I met her at a party at Alex's around Thanksgiving. She was there with a guy. She had on a dark top with a silver skirt, showing off her midriff. I had shlubby pants, a collared shirt with a T-shirt under it, and my calculator in my pocket.** I'd drunk three beers, which was enough to get me to talk to people.

I needed to call Mom (to tell her I'd arrived safely at "James's"), but I couldn't make the call on Alex's

*The church never called us teenagers, though, always "youth." We had "youth groups," "youth services," "youth Bible study," "youth ministry." St. John's loved that word.

**I always took my calculator everywhere, because whenever I left it at home, it got lost in my house, and then I couldn't find it when I needed it for school.

phone because the party was too noisy. So I began cruising for a cell phone. I figured I'd find some cool guy, borrow his phone, and huddle in a closet to talk with Mom. Instead, I ran into Judith; she was just finishing up a call out on Alex's porch.

"Excuse me, ah, hello, my name's Ned, and I was wondering if I could use that, your cell phone, for a second."

"Hi!" she said. She had such a happy little *hi*. It had a lot to do with my falling in love with her later on.

"Um, hello."

"Are you a friend of Alex's?" she asked.

"Since grade school."

"Oh! Well here, sure. The buttons work like this . . . " She drew herself close and showed me.

She was a gorgeous girl, and we talked for a while. Afterward, as I walked off the porch, Alex himself asked me if she was my girlfriend. I smiled. "I wish."

In the next two months, Judith dumped her boyfriend, got my phone number, and seeped into my life by showing up at events that I showed up at. It was confusing because she was so cool. Capital C Cool. It wasn't her money or her cell phone; it was the way she carried herself. She was a member in good standing of the Cool People. She went to another specialized public high school, but if she had gone to Stuy, I knew she'd be hanging out with Emily by the Snapple machine.

Our first date was a self-guided tour of a college both of us were looking at for next year. I don't know how I did it but, at some point, I got Judith into a secluded room, asked her out, and kissed her, all in rapid succession—all of which she was receptive to. Really.* I was James Bond for a day. Once the relationship began, though, I reverted to my bumbling self.

Physically, Judith was all smile. Her smile could thaw snowdrifts: perfectly spaced teeth, wide without being too wide, innocent, and *enthusiastic*, like she really wanted to see me, which was something I'd never experienced. She had brown eyes and brown hair; she duped me into thinking she was five feet five, with her sharp posture and high-heeled shoes, but she was actually five two. I got used to it. She had small glasses, small hands, small breasts—only her temper, as I came to learn, was ponderously massive.

Judith and I started going out January 26. Only a week into the relationship, we were talking every day—I called her from a pay phone at Stuy. She'd get

---

*This was all highly thrilling and unusual. At Stuy, I spent hours trying to dissect whether Girl A or B liked me; with Judith, it was clear from the beginning. All I learned during those high school musings was that if a girl likes you, she'll *look* at you a lot. That sounds obvious, but it works; you just have to know who's looking and who's daydreaming.

mad if the calls were less than ten minutes, so I'd bring extra quarters. During one of these conversations, I told her about Cancún.

"Ned, we have to make plans for your birthday."

"I'm not going to be around for my birthday. Didn't you know? I'm in Cancún from April second to April eighth, on the senior trip."

"Oh." That was something I'd learned to fear from Judith: the Clipped Oh. It meant trouble.

"Didn't I tell you about Cancún?"

"No."

Silence.

"I'm not going to cheat on you or anything," I lied. If the beach babe came along, I'd cheat on Judith in a flash.

"Oh, sure, you're not going to cheat on me, but you're going to get drunk a lot, aren't you?" Judith was always suspicious and judgmental about that stuff.

"No," I lied again.

"Oh."

More silence.

"I have to go," I said.

"Yeah, bye." Click. Judith was a fan of the hang-up-and-wait-for-Ned-to-call-back tactic. I ignored this volley, though, and went to class.

My life had become a two-front conflagration: on

one side, Judith—fighting with her, comforting her, and gradually falling in love with her; on the other side, playing Jesus.

The Easter Passion was run by Dale, a head honcho in the choir. Dale had some serious ambitions for our church. He wanted lavish costumes and tortured acting. He wanted to reveal the *soul* of Jesus. And he had written his own eleven-minute song, "I Saw Jesus," to anchor the show. (It was actually quite good.)

On the first day of rehearsal, I showed up alone so Dale could guide me step by step through the emotions of Jesus. "Ned, you have to understand that Jesus was a normal man. That's what's been lost in the centuries since he died. He wasn't a god, although he had God in him. He was just a man, with a man's fears and desires and hopes and faults. And you need to capture the difficulty of his decision—his decision to die."

"Okay."

"So you need to try this line again: 'Jerusalem, Jerusalem.' I don't want it to sound like Hamlet; I want it to sound like a normal man." I worked on that for a while; finally, after I told Dale that I was exhausted, he sent me home with some flyers.

"You can give these to people at your school." The flyers were yellow, with a stylish picture of the Son of

Man. They read, "Come to the Saint John's Passion Play, April 2, at 7:30 P.M."

I'd walked halfway home before it hit me: *April second, at seven thirty! April second!* That was when I was scheduled to leave for Cancún! I ran home and called Owen.

"Hey, dude, it's me. I have some questions for you about Cancún."

"What?"

"When does the plane leave?"

"April second, at eight thirty. Why?"

"Oh, man. I have to be Jesus on April second, at *seven thirty!*"

"*What?*"

"I need to play Jesus. In a church play. I'm sort of signed up for it."

"Dude, I don't know how, but you have to get out of that. If you don't make it on this trip, we are all screwed. Me, Josh, and Alex will have to pay more money, and we will all personally kill you."

"Okay, okay," I mumbled. "I'll get out of it."

I hung up the phone and went to Mom. "Sorry, I can't be Jesus," I said.

"*Whaaaat?*" You'd think my mother would get tired of this act, but no. She jumped off the couch and yelled, "You are *not* getting out of playing Jesus! You are committed to it, and you committed yourself to it, and it's a very important commitment! You cannot turn your back on your church that way!"

"But I have to be at James's country house on the day of the play!"

"No, you don't! That can wait. If you knew about that, you should never have agreed to play *Jesus!*"

I checked the apartment door; miraculously, it was closed.

"Mom, I didn't even want to play Jesus, y'know? You kind of made me do it, and now I'm telling you that I have to do something, and I can't be Jesus on the day I'm supposed to, and, uh, they'll have to find someone else." I was wavering, and Mom could tell.

"Absolutely not. You are still living under my roof, in my house, and you committed to something. If you cancel, you will be letting down a lot of very nice people."

"Well, if I don't leave April second, I'll be letting down a lot of nice people, too."

"Ned," Mom said, grabbing my cheeks like she used to do when I was six. "You are going to be in this play. That's *it.*"

"Okay," I said.

I walked slowly to my room. The last thing I needed now was to deal with Judith but, for some reason, I called her.

"Hey."

"Hi!" That was it. Her happy *hi;* I loved to hear it. "How are you?"

"Not so good. It looks like I can't go to Cancún."

"Oh. Why?"

"I have to be Jesus the same day."

Judith started laughing. She laughed for seconds, probably minutes. A minute of laughter is long on the phone.

"What's so funny?"

"Ned, you are *so* silly. You have—hold on." Laughter. "You have all these fantasies that you try to live out." More laughter. "You act like James Bond; you act like this rock star; and really, you're just playing Jesus in your church."

"Well, thanks," I smiled. "I'm glad you're so supportive of my hopes and dreams."

"Listen, *bubbelle.*" (That's what Judith called me when she was feeling happy.) "It's okay. It's—my God, it's bad enough that I'm not going out with a Jewish boy; now I have to tell my parents I'm with someone who's *playing Jesus.* Maybe it's good that you don't have to worry about that and Cancún at the same time."

"Yeah, maybe."

"What did your parents think about all this?" she continued.

"About Cancún?"

212

"Yes."

"Oh, I never told them."

Silence.

"What?"

"What?" I asked.

"You never told your parents you were going to Cancún?!"

"No. I, uh, had a plan. I was going to tell them I was at this guy James's house, see, and then I hoped they wouldn't call—"

"Are you *out of your mind?!* Who am I dating? Are you crazy? Really, Ned, are you a sane person? Can you think what would have happened if you had gotten hurt? If you needed help? Can you even imagine?"

"Uh, I guess so."

"This is ridiculous. You're ridiculous. Thank God you're not going to Cancún; you probably would have died."

"I don't think so."

"Jesus—wait, I'm talking to Jesus, aren't I?"

"Ha, ha."

"Ned, don't go doing crazy things. I care about you very much, and I don't want you going to Cancún and getting hurt. Okay?"

That's how it worked with Judith. First, the sucker punch—the "I-can't-believe-you're-such-a-jerk" chastising. Then the sweetness. It was a double whammy I could never fight. I'd convinced myself I wasn't going to Cancún because of playing Jesus, but I suppose I was doing it for her too.

I got off the phone, sat at the computer, and typed:

> **CANCÚN TICKET AVAILABLE**
> Hey, my name is Ned Vizzini and I can't go on the Cancún senior trip because I have to be Jesus (don't ask). I am giving away my ticket to whoever offers me the best stuff—TVs, a new car, whatever. Remember, the ticket is worth $850. I will take cash!

The next day, I posted copies of the announcement all over school, nearly crying as I stapled them to bulletin boards. There'd be no beach babe for me— no "Fun in the Sun."

I got three offers. A guy promised eight hundred dollars worth of marijuana; a girl offered enough Delta frequent-flier miles to go anywhere in the world for the next five years, and another guy presented a check for eight hundred fifty bucks. I took the check.

• • •

So I didn't lose anything. I got my money back, and I played Jesus as a normal man (with Mom watching, of course—she said I was inspiring, and she was proud to have me as her son). Then I spent my birthday with Judith—she didn't hand me a Corona with a wedge of lime, but she did say, "Hey, Ned, you're *eighteen!*" And she smiled very nicely.

Still, there's no rock song in that. I don't even think there's a lesson.

INTERLUDE

I honestly can't remember the second half of my senior year. I spent it all on Judith. She worked in Manhattan, and every few days I picked her up from work. She lived in far Brooklyn, and almost every day I went there on the subway to hang out in her bedroom. On days we didn't see each other, we always talked on the phone. Mom (again) thought I was on drugs, especially when I began ignoring her curfews altogether by coming home at midnight on weekdays, 5:00 or 6:00 a.m. on weekends. I guess I was in a bit of a daze; I lost a lot of weight and was tired all the time. But the stories stayed crystal clear.

• • •

I threw up on our first date. I had this great plan, see, to save money by eating at Burger King before we went out; then I would just order food for Judith. I figured that would be chivalrous, like a knight in shining armor getting a meal for his lady.

Well, Judith saw through me as we sat across from each other at King Wok's Chinese Cuisine. The waiter came by for our order.

"I'll just have tea," I said.

"You're not hungry?" Judith asked.

"Uh, not really," I told her.

"You're not hungry on our *first date?*"

Okay, so not eating was bad. I ordered some lemon chicken. It was way too much for my stomach, which was already dealing with a Whopper and onion rings; a half hour later, I found myself huddled over the King Wok toilet. I got some mints, though, from the cashier, and Judith never knew.

• • •

Our first fight took place in Barnes & Noble. We were hanging out there, and I checked my watch (actually, it was Mom's watch—she had lent it to me so I could get to a friend's Super Bowl party on time). Judith got mad because we were sort of in a back corner, and there'd been kissing; she felt it was ungracious of me to check the time. She stormed out of Barnes & Noble and I followed, totally unclear on what to do. I'd never seen a girl really mad before—at first I thought she was joking. We took two hours to settle the situation. I missed the Super Bowl party.

• • •

Another time, one of Judith's friends threw a birthday party at a blues club in Manhattan; Judith and I went.

I bought her an Irish coffee (seven dollars!), but when it arrived, it was too strong for her—more Bailey's than coffee—so she left it alone. Now, I wasn't going to waste seven of my dollars; I escaped to the bathroom with the coffee and downed it. Then I started worrying—what if she smelled the liquor on my breath? So I got out of the blues club and ran to a deli across the street for a stick of gum. While there, I noticed some green apples; I bought one of those instead, figuring it would clear up my breath just as well and be good for me. When I came back, Judith was livid. She wanted to know where I'd been for ten minutes, but mostly, she wanted to know what the hell I was doing in a blues club eating an apple.

• • •

I wanted a girlfriend all through high school, and when I finally got one, it was confusing and weird and stressful. But it also lived up to the hype, and that's rare. Pot didn't live up to its hype. Cigarettes didn't. Drinking didn't. The girl did.

PROM, PROM, PROMISES

Judith got me locked up for her prom early on. In fact, now that I think about it, that was one of the first things she did in our relationship. It happened in February. We were having our daily conversation, me at a pay phone at Stuy, her at home (she got out of school early).

"Ned, do you think we'll go to my prom together?" she asked innocently. Judith was so good at being innocent and sexy at the same time. She should've been outlawed.

"Uh, um, well, isn't your prom kind of in four months?"

Silence. "You don't think we'll still be boyfriend-and-girlfriend in four months?"

"Well, I don't know, I guess I, ah, I *hope* so." And I did. Judith was sweet; she was smart; I was getting attached to her, and this was a couple of days after my first half-fledged sexual encounter with anybody ever. I was kind of malleable.

"Well, haven't you *thought* about the prom?"

"Nope." I had never thought about the prom—not

since junior high, when I vowed to spend it alone watching football. I don't know why I vowed that; football season and prom season don't even coincide. But I had it in my mind from an early age that proms were not for me; proms were for other people, Cool People, and although I secretly wanted to attend, I'd never admit it.

"Well, Ned, you have to understand. Girls think about proms all the time. When a girl has a guy senior year, she always checks about the prom. You have to find *someone*. You don't want to be stuck at the last minute. Most girls have backups."

"Really?" I loved it when Judith gave the lowdown on how girls thought.* I had always been confused about how they thought, and she was so forthright. It shocked me.

"Oh sure, everyone I know has two or three people lined up for the prom. But I just want to go with you."

I could hear her smiling. She had me.

"What do I have to do?" I asked.

"Get a tux and a corsage."

"What's a corsage?"

"It's, like, a flower that goes around my wrist."

---

*Like when she told me, "Of course girls don't want to have sex! It hurts, the guys don't know what they're doing, and you could get pregnant. It's a lot better just to have some kind of reciprocal contact."

"Okay. No problem."

"And I have to get you a boutonniere. Which is a flower that goes in your tux."

"Okay. That sounds easy."

"Yeah, great, Ned. Why don't you try not to forget?"

"Yeah, yeah." I smiled. I don't know why she had me, but she did.

From then on, Judith's prom was a sacred pact between us. Basically, no matter how often we fought, how badly we fought, or what we fought about, we were committed to go to prom with each other.

Example: our first big fight took place in a department store on Judith's birthday. She wanted me to get some "nice clothes" so we could go dancing at "nice clubs." I was still viewing the relationship partly as an anthropology course; I'd never been to a dance club and I never thought I'd have the chance to go, so I was up for it. We went to Macy's and picked out a stylish shirt.

"That's gonna look really nice! Go try it on," Judith told me. I went to the changing room. There was a huge line.

"What's the deal?" I asked a guy in line. He was with his girlfriend as well. You can always spot the guys shopping with girlfriends: they have hangdog, embarrassed faces, and when they see each other, they give little smiles. You know, to help their brothers through their time of trial.

"I don't know," the guy said. "Someone's been in the room for like twenty minutes."

"Damn." I returned to Judith. "The changing room's occupied. I'm just gonna try this on right here." I began taking off my shirt to put on the new one.

"No!"

"What?"

"No! Don't do that!"

"What?"

"You can't just *try on a shirt in the middle of a store*. It's embarrassing. It's against the rules."

"It'll take a *second*. It doesn't make a difference."

"If you put that shirt on in here, I'm leaving."

Oh, boy. I put the shirt on. Judith stormed off. I followed her to the elevator, and we walked out of the store muttering at each other.

"You know what," I said as we stepped into the February night. "This is ridiculous. Why don't you just find somebody else to go to your prom, okay?"

Silence. We were silent for most of the walk to the subway, and most of the subway ride home, except for under-the-breath insults.

222

"There's plenty of girls who wouldn't care if I tried on a shirt in the middle of a store."

"Well, why don't you just go try and *find* them."

"Yeah, maybe I *will*, huh."

When the subway pulled into my stop, I decided things were over; Judith and I were clearly incompatible. I said bye, got up, and hustled out the train doors, leaving her by herself. I walked home thinking how nice the relationship had been, but how it was probably good that it was over.

As I entered the apartment, the phone rang.

"What the *hell* is wrong with you? You leave me like that on the *subway?* It's late at night and I'm wearing a skirt, and you leave me on the *subway?* Even if you don't like me anymore, you don't care about my *safety?* To *leave me on the subway?*"

"I'm sorry. I thought you *wanted* me to leave. I thought you said 'go.'"

"I didn't say *'go'!* My god, I don't even know where I *am* now, I'm walking toward your house; why don't you come out and meet me and give me money to take a car service home, if that's all you want to do. And then I'll leave you alone. You realize all this is happening *on my birthday!*"

"Okay, fine!" I went downstairs to give her money for a ride home, but that's not what ended up happening. What ended up happening was we started talking. She told me she had had such a nice time in the three weeks we were going out and that it was nicer than with any other guy before.

"You know what I was planning on saying to you today?" she choked as we sat on some stoop. "You know what I was practicing in my mirror this morning? 'I love you, Ned Vizzini. I love you, Ned . . .'" She started to cry.

I held her in my arms and told her I loved her, and we went to dinner. I did love her. Maybe I loved her because she loved me, which isn't the best reason, but I did love her, and in the ensuing months we spent almost every day together, and when it wasn't horrible, it was really, really good.

But that's all beside the point. The point was that, no matter *what* happened, we were going to Judith's prom. June 9. It was a contract, and it was binding, irrespective of love, incarceration, or grievous bodily harm.

• • •

Being a cheap and petty person, I was shocked at how expensive the modern prom is. There's a floor charge of a few hundred dollars—that's the price of two tickets, which are needed to get you and your date in the door. Then, unless you're some kind of bohemian, you need a limousine to arrive in style. You split the cost of the limo (i.e., rent a huge stretch limo for a bunch of couples), but no matter what, it's going to cost you—plus you have to tip the driver. Then the guy needs to rent a tuxedo, which is a nice round figure—one hundred dollars.* The girl needs a dress, which I won't even get started on: they seem to cost thousands of dollars.

Those are your basic prom expenses, but then there's the *after*-prom—an invention to keep drunk prom-goers from driving into telephone poles and impregnating each other. The idea is, once the prom ends, you go to *another* party, where you dance some *more;* then you go home around 8:00 A.M. The after-prom can be on a boat, a beach, or a rooftop, but it's going to cost you no matter where it is.

Three weeks before the prom, Judith started nagging me about my tux and corsage. Those were my only responsibilities, so you would think I had them under control, but no. On June 5, finally, with the same attitude I had starting an English paper at the last minute, I looked up "Tuxedos" in the Yellow Pages and found "Royal Crown." I called them and spoke to Marilyn, who sounded disturbingly like a grown-up Judith. I told Marilyn I

---

*A nod to the tuxedo industry. They make them cost one hundred dollars, so guys can remember easily.

needed a tuxedo for Thursday June 9, and she said it would be ready, but I was very lucky, because they only had one brand left, and a day later it would have been sold out.

Phew. No problem. Thursday June 9 rolled around; I went to school as usual, but when classes ended at 3:40, the marathon began. I ran out of American History and got home by 4:30. I packed a small bag of things I would need—deodorant and clothes for the after-prom—and left my house at 4:45. At 5:00, I dropped by a florist.

"Hey, I need a wrist corsage, with a white rose,"* I told the florist as I blundered in, making the little bell over the door go nuts.

The florist was a little European lady. "When do you need it by?" she asked calmly.

"Um, I kind of need it *now*, actually."

"Oh, well, we can't do now."

I panicked. "Well, I'm going to get my tux now. What about when I come back with my tux in about an hour?"

"*Hmmmm.*" Was this woman torturing me intentionally? "*Hmmmm*, yes, it can be done in an hour."

I paid her on the spot and got the hell out of there. At 5:35, I arrived at Royal Crown. Marilyn greeted me

---

*The color and style were per Judith's explicit instructions. She got the same style for my boutonniere.

at the door, a woman with *such* blond hair and *such* red lips that I was temporarily blinded.

"Hi, I'm Ned. I've come to pick up a tuxedo."

"Oh, *suuure*, Ned, right this way." She sat me down, got me my tux, and told me to try it on in the changing room. I took some deep breaths in there, unpacked the thing, and put it all on. A tux is like a Lego set, difficult at first, but the pieces fit together logically. I only had a problem with my cummerbund.

The cummerbund is this fat belt that goes around your waist and anchors your whole tuxedo getup. Unfortunately, my waist was a dainty thirty inches, so my cummerbund was way too loose. It just flapped around. Marilyn had to call some big guy named Johnny who worked in the back of Royal Crown. With several comments ("Damn, you're thin. You're really thin. You look so young. Are you really going to your *senior* prom? I've never seen anybody with less meat on their bones," etc.), he tightened my cummerbund to fit me. Satisfied, I walked toward the front door.

"Wait!" Marilyn screeched. "You're *leaving in the tux?!*"

"Isn't that what you're supposed to do?"

She smiled. "Have fun."

It was 6:30. I got some looks walking down the

street in a full tuxedo, but eventually, I made my way to the flower place and picked up the corsage.

"You have to keep it cold," the European lady told me. I saw why: there were frosty beads of water on the white flowers, perfect, as if they'd been placed there by an eyedropper.

"I'll do my best," I told her, blowing on it as I left the store. At 6:40, I got on the subway to Judith's.

I got a lot more looks riding the subway in a full tuxedo, but I put on my headphones so no one bothered me. I was listening to a song about leaving a bad relationship. I looped it over and over, vowing each time that once the prom was done, I would cool things off with Judith. From the beginning, I had promised her the prom, but we really weren't right for each other, and now I was delivering on my promise, and when I was finished delivering, I'd return to life as a fun-loving single guy.

I forgot all that when I saw her. She came to the door in a shimmering silver-blue dress, with her hair cut short and stylish, displaying her neck and shoulders. She had a small bag and high-heeled shoes, and a boutonniere for me. But above all, she was so *happy*. I'd never seen her so happy; her smile had weight to it. She hadn't even gone to school. She'd been home preparing all day.

"How do I look?" she asked.

"Gorgeous, gorgeous," I said, pulling her close. I would have kissed her, but I didn't because I knew it would ruin her makeup. We left her house and got in the limo.

I'd never been in a limo before, but it was much like I expected: TV, some drinks, a sunroof (that wouldn't open), a nice stereo system. The limo seated twelve people: Judith; her friends Alexis, Lisa, Katy, Michaela, and Girl Number Six; me, Charlie, Harris, and Guys Four through Six. Of the new people, only three were interesting: Charlie, Harris, and Michaela.

Charlie was Lisa's date, and it was clear from the start—even before he'd had any alcohol—that he was unhinged.

"Yo, I'm gonna effin'* go to the prom and get effed the eff up!" was what he said upon entering the limo. He slapped my hand. "What's your name?"

"Ned."

"Ned, man, that's a effin', that's a effin' name, yo." He sat down with Lisa. I didn't see them touch the whole night; maybe she just brought him along for comic relief. Charlie had a long, thin head and eyes that looked in different directions at the same time.

Michaela and Harris also provided entertainment. Michaela was one of those unfortunate girls

---

*Time for a little word association. I'm sure, if you're over the age of six, that you know what "eff" really means. The fine folks who first published this book told me that if I used the eff-word, I was effed and my book would never see the effing light of day. So just pretend.

who didn't get a backup date. She found herself stuck without anybody during the week of the prom, so she settled for Harris, a guy who clearly didn't want to be in the limo. From the beginning of the trip, Michaela and Harris fought; an hour into the prom, they were sitting as far away from each other as possible, glaring.

The limo drove slowly through Brooklyn, picking people up. Guys Four through Six, like Charlie, were interested in getting "effed the eff up." I would've liked to get a little effed, too, but Judith had a vise grip on all that.

"You're not going to get drunk, right, Ned?"

"No, no, I'm not." I didn't mind, really. I figured I'd need all my wits about me to navigate the prom successfully and emerge at its end with some kind of sex.

I was still a virgin. That was something I worried about every day; something I had worried about since I was thirteen or fourteen; something that particularly worried me because the average American male loses his virginity at sixteen. I was two years behind. I had lied about that so many times, to so many different people, that I could never keep my stories straight. Ike thought I'd had sex when I was sixteen; Hector and James believed I'd done it a month earlier with Judith—even Judith herself was under the impression that I'd slept with someone about a year before, probably the only time in history a guy has lied to a girl about sex *in that direction*.

I was totally dense with Judith and sex. Three weeks into the relationship, I asked her if I should show up with condoms the next time we saw each other. She cried for hours. "You think I'm that much of a *slut*? Is *that* why you're so nice to me?" I held her for a long time to calm her down. "You're not a slut; I'm just an idiot," I said over and over.

Now, four months later, at her prom, Judith was beginning to suspect my virginity, because after the initial condom fiasco, I never talked about sex. I did an about-face; I felt so bad about being high-pressure that I became no-pressure, never discussing it, never bringing it up. It scared the hell out of me. I didn't know what was going to happen at the prom, but if we had some reciprocal contact by the end of the night, I'd be happy.

See, Judith had estranged me from my sexual nemesis: television. All the time I was with her, I was so busy running around New York, picking her up from work, buying her gifts, and calling her, that I never watched TV. And when you don't watch TV— when you divorce yourself from the oversexed teenagers the programmers throw at you—you feel a lot better about your own sex life, or lack of one.*

• • •

We arrived at Judith's prom around 8:30; it was in the lobby of the Marriott Hotel in downtown Brooklyn. It looked just like a prom from the movies: the guys were in tuxes standing outside the Marriott, smoking; the girls traveled in little groups to and from the bathroom, giggling. Photographers were set up in the lobby, and teachers milled about in suits and dresses hitting on each other.

Judith led me in, introducing me to people she knew from school, whose names I quickly forgot. I found a sort of cocktail room, where I pigged out on chicken fingers being served on little trays before Judith showed me to the main room, with tables and a dance floor.

My inability to dance had by now become a serious phobia; in fact, the first time Judith had taken me dancing, I threw up. Everything was going fine. I was out on the floor with her, and she was smiling, looking splendid under the black light . . . then I saw myself in the mirrored ceiling and got sick. I excused

*This is my only complaint about TV. I don't think it causes violence; I don't think it promotes low morals; and truthfully, I don't care about low morals. I just hate TV for making me feel like I have to have sex with hundreds of interesting people to have a normal life.

myself, ran to the bathroom, and retched in a toilet repeatedly.* I just looked so stupid in that mirror: I was the prototypical white guy without rhythm. I could tap rhythms in my head and play rhythms on my bass guitar, but when it came to moving rhythmically, I was a complete bust.

Judith didn't care. She wanted to dance, and she continued dragging me to clubs. I developed a method to keep from vomiting: I'd hum Led Zeppelin tunes. Led Zeppelin is the ultimate alpha-male band. When you hum their songs, you're tapping into an underlying male world energy, and it helps you through tough situations. I would be dancing like mad with Judith, lips moving a mile a minute, mouthing the lyrics to "Black Dog" or "Whole Lotta Love."**

At the prom, however, I found another way to beat my dancing phobia: *waxed floors*. When Judith took me up to groove, I noticed immediately how slippery the floor was. I could slide back and forth on my toes like James Brown! I got so into it that I forgot about how dumb I looked and just danced, which is what you're supposed to do at a prom.

"I love you," Judith whispered. I whispered the

---

*I got a lot of sympathetic looks from Cool Club Guys as I puked. "It'll be okay," one dude with slick black hair told me. If only he knew the cause.

**Led Zeppelin is pretty much acknowledged as being the best hard rock band of all time. Also, they had a jet.

same back and meant it. I also told her she looked gorgeous. She did. She was the best-looking girl in the building.

• • •

By 11:30, the prom was over and the after-prom began. Our crew—Judith, Alexis, Lisa, Katy, Michaela, Girl Number Six, me, Charlie, Harris, and Guys Number Four through Six—piled into the limo and drove off to a dance club called Metropolis. Harris and Michaela were fuming, and it was clear that Charlie and Guys Number Four through Six had gotten their hands on some mind-altering substances.

"Yo, man, my effin' dog, his name is Jake! And I got this effin' other dog, his name is Jake, too! What the eff kind of effin' idiot people do I live with, to name both dogs the same thing? You call one dog, the other one comes—"

That was Charlie. He had me in stitches the whole night.

"I'm not talking to her. I got nothin' to say to her." That was Harris, in one corner of the limo, glaring at Michaela, in the opposite corner. "I have nothing to say to you either, *thankyouverymuch!*" she snapped.

"Yo," Guy Number Five said. "Let's tear it up." The limo was stuck in traffic on the Brooklyn-Queens Expressway. The cars were moving at about three miles per hour. This gave Guy Number Five the idea of throwing open the limo door, jumping out, running around in traffic, and peeing on an abandoned car. Guy Number Four, Guy Number Six, and Charlie followed.

We got to Metropolis at 1:00 A.M.* It was huge, a refurbished warehouse with a giant neon sign and a snaking line out front. Somehow (Guy Number Five had a connection), we bypassed the line and got into the club.

Pulsing music, bright lights, body heat—dance clubs always made me think of rats, and the experiments scientists do to put them into sensory overload. Our group quickly split up, with Charlie and Guys Number Four through Six pinpointing the beer. I stayed close to Judith. The nasty thing about these places was that unless you stayed with your girlfriend at all times, guys would randomly touch her, and then you'd have to start a fight which, despite those years at True Power Martial Arts, I was not equipped to do.

"Buy me a drink?" Judith asked. This was her thing: ask for a drink and then drink one-quarter of it. She didn't like alcohol—she liked the appearance of a glass in her hand.

"I'm out of money," I said casually.

---

*Ninety minutes to get there? That's right; when you're in traffic in New York, and people are periodically jumping out of your limo to urinate, it can take some time to reach your destination. It didn't help that Metropolis was way out in Queens.

"What?"

I figured she couldn't hear me over the dance music. "I said I'm *out of money.*"

"I can hear you, you idiot! Why the *hell* are you out of money?!"

"Well, it's all gone: tux, corsage, paying the limo guy."

"Ned! You were supposed to bring money *in addition* to all that stuff!"

"Oh, geez, well, I'm sorry."

"This night is *not over!* This is my *prom!* I'm staying out until eight in the morning. So you had better find some money."

Judith stormed off. I sat by myself at the side of the club, my worst fears confirmed. Judith wanted her prom to be like the movies; she wanted me to come over, pick her up, and whisk her through the night with everything taken care of, no complications. And if I had been the right kind of guy, the kind who goes to the bank and says, "Damn, it's my girlfriend, who I love, let me take out a bunch of cash," I could have made her prom as good as she'd imagined. Instead, I was a disaster.

I'd been sitting there ten minutes when Judith came back. Smiling.

"Someone bought me a drink," she said coyly.

"Really?"

"That's right. Some *guy* bought me a drink. And it *wasn't* you." She pointed at my nose.

"Well, why don't you go dance with the guy, then?" I offered.

"Nope." She sat in my lap.

"Why not?"

"Because I'd rather be here with you." She wasn't drunk. Judith never got drunk. She had just *changed moods*. Like I'd seen her do so many times before.

"C'mon, kiss me, it's my prom," she said. I thanked whatever god was responsible and kissed her as well as I could.

• • •

We were at Metropolis until around 3:30; things blurred from there. The limo drove us to not one, but two diners, where I borrowed money to pay for Judith's food. I started drifting asleep around 5:00 A.M., while we were still driving around. Judith reacted to this by flirting with some other guy ("Oh yeah, that's my boyfriend, the one *asleep* back there"). Guys Number Four through Six disappeared; I don't know where they went; Harris and Michaela never settled things. Charlie kept talking nonstop, using the eff-word more and more frequently, hitting strides where he was able to make every noun, verb, adjective, and adverb an eff-derivative. Then he passed out on the floor of the limo. I just held Judith and kept my mouth shut. I had nothing to say.

At 7:30 A.M., the limo dropped us off at her house. I couldn't tip the guy, but I'm sure the other people tipped him enough.

"You want to come up?" Judith asked. I was holding her hand, crossing her street, approaching her apartment building. I nodded.

Her parents were still asleep, so we went to Judith's room. I took off her shoes and rubbed her feet. I rubbed her back, her arms, her legs, her hands. She was sore from all the dancing. She lay down in her bed and I rubbed her neck and told her I loved her. I kissed her cheeks and her arms . . . and I realized how wrong I'd been.

Contractual obligation? Nah. This girl, who'd come into my life like a whirlwind—not caring that I was six feet, one hundred *forty-three* pounds—didn't think of her prom as a contractual obligation. She'd sealed me up for it early on because she wanted it perfect, like in the movies, and I'd nearly ruined it. In fact, I had ruined it. She'd brought it back from the dead by smiling at me.

So shut up, Ned. Shut up and think about someone else for a change. Shut up and rub the girl's back
and try—I know it's hard—to make her prom as important in your mind as it is in hers. Try not to be
such a cynical eff.

HOOTERS

In the summer after senior year, I took my last cheap East Coast vacation with my family. This time, we had a van with *three* backseats (two just wasn't enough for Daniel, Nora, and me), and we found ourselves in Charleston, West Virginia.

"Here we go, folks, 'Entering Charleston,'" Dad said, reading the road sign. He already loved West Virginia because the posted speed limit was seventy miles per hour, which meant he could do his usual ninety with less anxiety.

"You kids should know some things about West Virginia," Mom proclaimed from the passenger seat, twisting around to face us.

"What should we know about West Virginia, dear?" my father asked sarcastically as he zoomed past a truck.

"You shush," Mom said. "I'm talking to the kids."

"Yes, well, I guess I'll just keep on driving silently. Sorry, dear."

My mother sighed. "You see what he does to me? He's the king of patronizing, your father."

Dad began reciting a poem very loudly, gesturing wildly with both hands as he hit the gas.

"Ignore him," Mom said. "Now, West Virginia is the poorest state in the country; I mean, it has the lowest average income. The main industry is still coal—"

"Whoa!" My fourteen-year-old brother saw it first.

At the side of the road was a billboard for Hooters.

"Hooters!" Daniel yelled. "Oh my gosh! Look, it's only fifteen miles away! Dad, can we go to Hooters? Can we? Can we?"

The billboard showed a blonde with immense breasts.* It said simply: "Hooters—The Cure for the Common Restaurant."

Now, I've always admired Hooters. Some back-woods mountain kid probably started it on a bet, and it's become a multimillion-dollar franchise, with restaurants in New York, L.A., Fargo, Albuquerque. Plus, it advertises young, buxom, pretty waitresses in short shorts and tight shirts. I chimed in with Daniel: "Yeah, Dad, can we go to Hooters?"

"Uh," Dad slowed down for a turn; the speedometer dipped under seventy. "I don't think your mother would approve . . ."

---

*Of course, they were immense on the billboard, but even if this woman were shrunk to scale and paraded down the street, they'd still be immense.

"Oh please, Jim," she waved a hand at him. "It's local color. Of course you can go. I don't care one whit."

Two hours later, after checking into our hotel, Dad, Daniel, and I rolled into Hooters. Mom and Nora stayed behind to watch a romantic comedy on Pay-Per-View.

"Dad, you cannot wear that," I pleaded for the twentieth time as we entered the Hooters parking lot. My father had on his best blazer and tie.

"When I eat dinner, I get properly dressed for it," he retorted. "Just because we're going to this *particular* establishment doesn't mean we have to dress badly."

"Please," I begged, looking into Hooters from the van. The patrons were wearing jeans and lumberjack shirts. "Dad, c'mon. You look like a pretentious idiot. Just drop the blazer."

Reluctantly, he draped it over the driver's seat.

We hopped out of the van and strolled into the restaurant. It was like a gigantic log cabin. The ceiling was about twenty feet high, holding industrial-strength lights* and fans. The walls were wood grain, with pictures of bikini-clad girls and humorous posters. ("Caution: Blondes Thinking!" Ha ha.)

---

* Keeping the place well lit probably cut down on the number of "incidents" with waitresses, and it helped distinguish Hooters from the common strip club.

A blonde came up to us. She was pretty in a scary, done-up way. She wore about a half-inch of makeup, and I wondered how she kept it from melting under the Hooters glare. Carrying that steamy, greasy food must be murder on eyeliner. Her name tag said, "Crystal H." I wondered if there was a "Crystal G."

"Three?" Crystal H. asked us with a tight Southern twang.

"Yes," Dad answered. His voice was about three octaves below hers.

"Okay!" She led us to our table. We were surrounded by TVs; Hooters had eleven or twelve of the largest televisions I'd ever seen, blaring baseball on ESPN and football on ESPN2.

Crystal took our drink orders. "Hello and welcome to Hooters. You should know we have a very large selection of beers: Amstel, Budweiser . . ." She listed brands alphabetically for nearly a minute. I thought it was a real feat of memory until I noticed she was reading from a list.

"Do you have Rolling Rock?" Dad asked.

"Ooh, no, sorry!"

"Becks?"

"Oh, sir, you keep naming beers we don't have!"

"Heineken?"

"Yes, we have that. And for you two?"

"Coke," Daniel and I said in unison.

Crystal folded up her pad. "Y'all aren't from around here, are you?"

"No, we're from Brooklyn, actually," I said.

"Oh, wow! I thought so. Are you Italian? You look Italian."

"Yes," Dad said.

"And how old are you?" Crystal asked Daniel and me, cocking her head.

"Eighteen," I answered.

"Fourteen," Daniel mumbled. He was watching "Thirty Years of the Detroit Lions" on ESPN2.

"Eighteen?" Crystal gasped at me. "My gosh, I thought you were *fifteen.* You look so *young.* Do you Italians always look that *young?*"

"Uh . . ." I didn't know what to say.

"I mean, I'm *nineteen,*"* Crystal continued. "You really don't look eighteen. I thought you were about fifteen, really."

"Well, sorry," I shrugged.

"Okay, I'll be back with y'all's drinks." She walked away.

"Geez," I grabbed my head. People always think I look young, or act young. I'm going to be that idiot who has to show his I.D. when he's thirty, not

---

*I thought she was twenty-five. I'm horrible with ages, just like I'm horrible with names. If they're past the age of twelve, I can't tell whether people are thirteen or thirty.

because he looks young and virile but because he's so doofy no one will believe he's an adult.

Crystal returned with our drinks and took our food orders, tapping her pen impatiently on her pad. There was a burly man dressed in black leather seated at a table in the back whom she was eager to talk to. Whenever she stopped dealing with us, she went right to him. Throughout the night, I tried to figure out whether he was a paying customer, her boss, or just some guy she liked.

"I'd like the buffalo wings—Three-Mile Island, please?" I said. The wings came in medium, hot, and Three-Mile Island.

"Ooh, honey, are you sure that won't be too hot for you?" Crystal asked, alarmed.

"I like hot stuff," I seethed. "I'll be fine."

"*Ooookay.*" She tiddled off to get the food, after making a pit stop at the burly guy.

I was beginning to see how Hooters worked. It wasn't that the waitresses were pretty: some were, but some looked like plastic surgery gone wrong. It was that they talked to you; they were *paid* to talk to you; they did so enthusiastically, with smiles. Hooters taps into the deep-down loneliness of the American male.

And the place was almost 100 percent men. We

did see one couple* and one mother-son pairing. Dad and I discussed what kind of kid would go to Hooters with his mom, and what his nickname would be when the murders began.

The conversation cheered me up, and as the night wore on, I forgot about Crystal's remarks and got into the Hooters atmosphere: the laid-back, TV-watching, oh-wow-there's-some-cleavage, bright, safe sleaze of the place. I ate some Three-Mile wings and polished off a cheeseburger. I watched ESPN, talked with my brother, and almost convinced Dad to buy me a beer. Toward the end of the night, I even connected with Crystal on a subject: Conan O'Brien, the late-night TV host.

"Yeah, I met him once," I told her as she refilled my Coke. "I saw him on the street and shook his hand. He's actually very tall."

She stopped dead: "*No.* Conan O'Brien is *tall?*"

"Oh, sure, he's about six feet four."

"I don't believe you."

"I'm dead serious. The other guy on the show, his sidekick, is six feet, and Conan makes him look small. He's a very tall man."

"My gosh, I never knew that. I'm gonna tell all my

---

*The girl looked happy, the guy, thrilled; I guess when you find someone who'll go to Hooters with you, it's true love.

friends, and *none* of them are gonna believe me." She walked away shaking her head, "Conan O'Brien is *tall!*"

Around 11:00 P.M., two hours after our arrival, we were still staring at a lot of food. I couldn't finish my wings; Daniel had hardly touched his; and Dad, who could've eaten everything on our table plus a milk shake, was holding back as part of a diet. Crystal noticed our leftovers and came over with Styrofoam containers, which she loaded with notable grace. "I know you think you're never going to be hungry again, because you ate so much," she chided, "but believe me, later on, you *will* be hungry again and you'll want to eat this!"

Minutes later she gave us the check. Actually, she gave *me* the check and glanced at me appreciatively. I looked down at it. She had written, "Very nice meeting you and I hope that you enjoyed wild and wonderful WV. Crystal." With a smiley face. I guess that's something they make all the Hooters girls write.

Dad, Daniel, and I made our way to the van; as soon as we were out of Hooters, we felt comfortable rating it.

"I liked that," Daniel said. "It was, like, TV and girls. Together."

"I don't know," said Dad. "You can get tired of places like that."

"Yeah," I mumbled. "You can."

But that wasn't what I was thinking. I was thinking about Crystal—how awful it was to be near her when it was her *job* to talk to me, and how much nicer it would've been if she had *wanted* to talk to me. I was thinking how fake it all felt.

I was thinking about loneliness, adulthood, my girlfriend situation, college, and how final this all was—the last family vacation, maybe the last night-time parking-lot walk with my father and brother, for a while anyway. When I got in the van, I convinced Dad to play my live AC/DC tape, and we drove back to the hotel, rocking out.

POST–HIGH SCHOOL

When *Teen Angst? Naaah . . .* was published, some of my friends questioned the ending. "It just . . . ends," they told me. I responded, "It's life! Life doesn't have tidy endings," but I understood their frustration. Now, years later, I have the chance to tack on a tidy ending, and it's tempting to say that our class lived happily ever after.

But the truth is, I haven't kept in touch with the vast majority of people from my high school. I think that's a good thing, as I didn't *like* the vast majority of the people from my high school: the ones from the student union, the self-righteous computer nerds, the women . . . Only the most important ones have stuck around, and they were the ones who had already made it into this book anyway.

Ike, my self-declared vampiric Mayan friend, traveled for a while. The last time I saw him was in his house in Brooklyn. Ike had become involved with "perfect black." Black dyes, see, are not truly black. They reflect light to an infinitesimal degree. And a small but dedicated group of chemists and fashion researchers are attempting to eliminate this, to achieve perfect, total black. A noble quest, and one I wish him well on.*

I still keep in touch with James, my soft-spoken, trench-coat-wearing friend. (He has stopped wearing trench coats.) Among other things, he managed to get a professional electronic drum set rigged up to Rock Band, the rock music video game that has made all of my youthful musical ventures obsolete. He started playing the game with the real drum set and within a few months *taught himself how to play drums using Rock Band.* Then he took his guitar, bass, and vocal abilities and recorded a demo. Here's hoping someone reads this and offers him a record deal. Maybe we can tour together!

Poppy, who gave me my summer of dominoes and beer, is long gone from East Fourth Street. For better and worse, New York has become so safe and so expensive since this book was written that the unconquerable downtrodden people who taught me so much about life—Poppy, Old Franky/Old Tony, Aeneas, Husky and Lanky, Major—were priced out, forced into other lifestyles, or (I somehow know) sucked into death.

I haven't talked to Judith in a decade.

My family is wonderful, all alive, and, as Dad

---

*Also, after having misplaced it for a number of years, I found the Wormwhole demo Ike and I made! It's available for free at www.nedvizzini.com/fun/#music.

says, none of us duds. I do my thing, which although sometimes dudlike can't be entirely written off. Danny got into applied math, aka math that is *completely crazy;* my sister grew into the most practical, implacable person I know.

My mother is happy. When we children left the house, she got dogs, and even though she's a vegetarian, she loves the dogs so much that she rips up roast chicken into bite-sized strips to feed them. But I know that the dogs are just a stopgap until I give her grandchildren. Then I'm going to see some *real* coddling.

Regarding my father: a friend of his told him that *Teen Angst? Naaah . . .* is really a love story about him. I can see why. He appears in this book as a guide, a friend, a leader, a sage. He's still truckin'. He's still hilarious. He still likes rock music, although he likes jazz better. But most of all, he still tells stories better than anyone I know. The only thing is, he can't *write* them. That's a big reason I write them.

As for me, I've been through lots of dramatic flare-ups since this book was written but ultimately had an incredible, ridiculous life. After *Teen Angst? Naaah . . .* was published, I went to college and got an idea for a novel about a guy who takes a pill that makes him cool. That book was published a few years later; it's called *Be More Chill.*

When I signed the contract to write *Be More Chill*, though, it wasn't just for one book—it was for two. I proceeded to go (certifiably) crazy trying to write book number two. The thing about writing is that sometimes the stories *don't* come; sometimes you sit there wondering how they *ever* came. That's when you realize why it made sense to the Greeks to just think that there were Muses, and they came or went based on their own schedules, and if they didn't come, you couldn't write. When I look back at this book and see tales about a street punk named Aeneas singing "I got no money today / Because I run-ied away," I can't do anything but believe that a Muse was watching out for me.

In any case, the Muses weren't coming after *Be More Chill*. I wrote half a book but watched it die on the vine. I can explain exactly what that's like. Have you ever had a bad haircut? And you know as you're getting the haircut that it's no good, but you keep hoping, "Maybe there's some master plan here. Maybe this person really knows what they're doing." And you want to speak up, but that would be embarrassing, and then, all of a sudden . . . it's over. And you've got a bad haircut.

That's what it's like to write a bad book.

So one night, I just couldn't deal with this whole failed writing thing. I got up and called the Suicide

Hotline. They told me to go to the nearest psych hospital.

For the next week or so, I had the most intense and amazing experience of my life, with people who changed my perspective on everything. After I got out, I wrote about it. That turned into my third book, *It's Kind of a Funny Story.*

And that book satisfied the contract!

• • •

I had a lot of jobs after college—silly jobs like bike messenger and computer programmer—and part of me always worried that the money from writing would dry up and I'd never escape my parents.* Now, however, anything else is not an option. My resume is all over the place; it looks like the resume of a seagull. I'm a writer from now on, for better or worse, and so far it's mostly all better.

Do I have days where I wake up and no Muses are there and I don't even want to deal with my *life* anymore? Sure. Do I have days where I learn that something—some speaking engagement, some meeting, some project—has been canceled, or I've missed some opportunity, and I want to hit myself in the head for being such a dope? Sure. But above and beyond that are the days when the words come together

*I have gotten out of my mother's ZIP code! (Though I do still reside within her area code.)

and I sit back in my chair and go, "Man, this is fun."
And there are the days where I get an e-mail or a letter from someone who read my writing and liked it
and I just slap myself in the head for an entirely different reason, because I'm blessed.

Thank you. Thank you, Mom, Dad, Daniel, Nora, readers, Muses, Margaret. Thank you, all the people who published this stuff, every teacher and librarian who's ever asked me to speak; thank you to the U.S. Post Office for allowing me to send my books cheaply. Thank you, you reading this, you.

Thank you, Hostess Cupcakes and coffee yogurt.

INDEX